ADVANCE PRAISE FOR DECIDE SUCCESS

"John Baumann has used his life as an example and inspiration for others to follow. Decide Success offers wisdom and confidence on how to make the most out of your life and find happiness and fulfillment every step of the way. After you read it, you will say: What a book!

—John Y. Brown Jr., 55th Governor of Kentucky

"What an amazing book. The best thing you can do for your personal and professional development is to read this book. So deciee for yourself to succeed and read John's book."

—G.J. Hart, CEO of California Pizza Kitchen, former CEO of Texas Roadhouse

"John Baumann has taken on the biggest questions any of us can face (What do I want out of my life? How can I achieve it?) and described twelve specific, concrete steps that will lead each of us to the answers. These answers will, of course, be different for every reader, but John demonstrates that the process by which we arrive at them is not. Read this book with pen in hand; you will want to highlight the many nuggets of wisdom and return to them often as you work John's method to conquer the world, or at least your corner of it."

—Matthew Hamel, Executive Vice-President, Brown-Forman Corporation

" It is extremely well written, and filled with practical and useable advice supported by entertaining real life examples. The book is uplifting, energetic, enriching and inspirational. It provides a clear, common sense roadmap to improvement and success on all levels – professional and personal."

—Chris Campbell, Senior Vice President, YUM BRANDS

"I have been reading your book and I love the vision and passion you convey to your audience. The value is in understanding the basic rules of engagement and to better one's outcome if they seize on your basic principles. Thank you for sharing your personal journey, it is truly inspirational."

—T. Vernon Foster, Director, University of Louisville Business Solutions

D1403637

"John Baumann's passion for self-realization is contagious. Go ahead. Read this book and be everything you can be."
—Debra Hoffer, President, Junior Achievement of Kentuckiana

"In his book, Decide Success: You Ain't Dead Yet, John Baumann has written a terrific guide to living deliberately. Intended to inspire people with Parkinson Disease to move forward and forego the temptation to think their life is over, through humor, personal experience and touching revelation he presents a methodology for success in dealing with chronic disease."

His common sense analysis of the steps necessary to turn tragedy into opportunity and the methods to implement those steps, applies to anyone who is in need of direction and focus. I wonder how much more successful all our lives would be had we developed these habits as young people? It is good to know there's still time because 'We ain't dead yet!'"
—Pamela Kell, Parkinson's Creative Collective

DECIDE

SUCCESS

You Ain't Dead Yet

Twelve Action Steps to
Achieve The Success
You Truly Desire

John M. Baumann, BBA, JD
Faculty, University of Louisville, College of Business
National Speakers Association Inspirational Speaker
Success Workshop Facilitator
Parkinson's Proud since 2002

DECIDE SUCCESS: You Ain't Dead Yet

www.theinspiringesquire.com

This book is manufactured in the United States.

Unattributed quotes are by John Baumann.

© Copyright 2011 John Baumann
SECOND EDITION 2013

Publisher:
JK Success Enterprises, LLC
Louisville, KY 40245

ISBN
Soft Cover 978-0-9834165-0-0

Baumann, John
    DECIDE SUCCESS: You Ain't Dead Yet

Bulk Orders:
Quantity discounts are available on bulk purchases of this book for educational and training purposes. Discounts are also available to organizations, schools, libraries, corporations and others. To learn more, contact JohnDecideSuccess@gmail.com.

Dedication

To my Grandpa Al DeLuca, my goombah, whose unconditional love and influence I can still feel today over thirty years after his soul moved on.

Acknowledgements

I want to thank the following people for all their assistance, inclusion and/or encouragement: Joe for his perspective, Katie for her courage, Peggy for her guidance, Pop for his positive outlook, Randy for his graphic talent, Rich for his "cabin," Rochelle for her enthusiasm, Susan for her tirelessness, and especially, my Mom, Mary Agnes DeLuca Baumann, my biggest supporter. I needed you all to successfully create this book.

I also want to send a very special thank you to my love, my wife, Bernadette, for saving my life in so many ways. This book was written before we met, at least in this lifetime, but, most certainly, was inspired and influenced by the image that I always had of you and your unbelievably beautiful and resilient spirit. Absolute Love.

Contents

THE WORK PHASE

Chapter 3: Putting Forth Your Best Effort

Chapter 4: Preparing and Practicing

Chapter 5: Raising Your Level of Intensity

THE ACTIVE PHASE

Chapter 6: Seeking Out Experiences

Chapter 7: Developing Contacts and Resources

THE EXPANSION PHASE

Chapter 8: Increasing Your Level of Awareness

Chapter 9: Trusting Your Instincts

THE LEGACY PHASE

Chapter 10: Maintaining a Positive Attitude

Chapter 11: Uncompromising Integrity

Chapter 12: Having Faith

Chapter 13: Applying the Twelve Action Steps

Introduction
What can you do to be more successful?

My mother had said to me hundreds of times, "Everything happens for the best." Almost a year after I was diagnosed with Parkinson's sitting in her living room having casual conversation, her favorite commentary changed. "Well, remember John, everything happens for a reason." What had always been the "best" was now a mediocre "reason", solemn and unexplainable "reason"?

When I confronted her about it, she reluctantly explained, "I can't imagine that your Parkinson's Disease is for the best." I felt a sudden rush. I didn't know it then, but I had been looking for something to inspire me. Right then and there, I made the decision to give her optimistic "best" back. Somehow, some way, I would make my having Parkinson's "for the best."

The fog and denial that I had been living in started to lift. I felt a purpose. That's why I wrote this book.

I was a successful student and professional. The same principles and steps I used to develop my life then apply equally to living life to the fullest after a life-changing event. Your own medical condition or one of a loved one, personal loss, change in your job or even relationship situation can suddenly stop you in your tracks and change the your life as you had known it to be. It does not have to break you. You can make it "for the best".

If you think that being diagnosed with Parkinson's is the best thing that happened to me. The answer is no. Having unlimited amount of money, traveling the world first class, having and occasional dinner with my favorite Red Sox player,

Carl Yastrzemski, that could be the best thing that could happen to me.

But you could ask how can anyone be so upbeat? Be so optimistic? Knowing they have an incurable, progressive, neurologic, debilitating disease? At 41 years young?" Is it possible for someone to have had a "so called" great life with a successful career in the field that he loves, in a life style that he loves, suddenly taken away from him. Yet remain uninterrupted. Strong. Happy. Almost superhuman.

That answer is a definite "yes," but most of the time. Sometimes I get sad. I am pissed off at times. I sometimes feel scared. I know what the long-term looks like. I have seen people diagnosed with Parkinson's "not doing so well." It would be a lie if I said I didn't put myself in those shoes for a millisecond.

At times, I need to lean on my Bernadette. Reminding myself to "Let go and let God." I have to force myself to bring my focus back to what is now and follow my "life purpose." Then I can be the person you see in my inspirational talks. The voice you hear when you read this book. The person you talk to one-on-one and look to for hope. The enthusiastic, passionate and inspirational person who is John Baumann.

It's through pain and fear that builds a warrior. That's why you fight. There is not a person throughout history that made a difference who did not have to fight. I see the fear in the eyes of the people in my audiences. They want to fight, but need guidance to find their mission. They find peace in my words of hope. I am determined to make my Parkinson's "for the best" and I will succeed. Make the decision. DECIDE SUCCESS. I live the title of my book.

And, by the way, I ain't dead yet.

Who am I? I graduated from Cornell Law School in 1986 and *summa cum laude* from the University of Massachusetts School of Business. I worked as an attorney from 25 years including as top lawyer for a NASDAQ-listed company. I am on the faculty of the University of Louisville School of Business. I am also the Chair of the Make-A-Wish Kentucky Board and have been Parkinson's Proud since 2002. I have provided inspirational talks to groups including in Texas, Alabama, Vermont, Missouri, Florida, Oklahoma, Kentucky, New York, Ohio, Illinois, North Carolina, Indiana, St. Thomas in the Virgin Islands and several locations in Canada.

DECIDE SUCCESS uses short stories to bring the success principles to life, engaging imagery. I have dedicated my life to inspiring, explaining my twelve action steps to achieve the success you truly desire to, and bringing hope to as many people as possible. You will have an actual plan *to be more successful* after reading this book.

There are twelve action steps to achieve the success that you truly desire. I make no secret of the phases and steps:

1. Part I (the Mapping Phase) is to assess and envision;
2. Part II (the Work Phase) is to give your best effort, prepare, and raise your level of intensity;
3. Part III (the Active Phase) is to seek out experiences, and identify and nurture contacts and resources;
4. Part IV (the Expansion Phase) is to increase your level of awareness and to trust your instincts; and
5. Part V (the Legacy Phase) is to maintain a positive attitude, live a life of integrity, and have faith. These are in a very specific sequential, step-by-step order.

I want to mention that there is a real reason that I included the phrase, *you truly desire.* Sometimes what you believe you desire to be successful is not what you truly desire.

This book starts and ends with these twelve principles. The guts of this book explain and add flesh to these principles. I used to think that success was something reserved for a person starting out and then establishing a career, but there are so many more applications for these success principles. Some have decided to focus their attention to succeed in a sport or an artistic endeavor whether as a career or as a hobby. Success comes in a variety of shapes and sizes.

My most recent decision to succeed was in the area of public speaking and, I guess, writing as is evidenced by this book. Before that, my most significant decision to succeed was to live the fullest life possible with Parkinson's Disease. The twelve action steps to achieve success have as much applicability in starting a new career as they do to positively handling an incurable illness.

Many of the examples and illustrations in this book are drawn from my own personal experiences. This is not meant to be an autobiography or a self-testimonial. However, I have learned many valuable lessons from my life experiences that I am sharing with you so that you better understand the principles and can learn from the stories.

Let me explain the title. I started with *Twelve Steps to Success,* moved to *Decide to be more Successful,* then to *Decide to Succeed,* and finally settled on the shortest version of all, *Decide Success,* because that says it all in as concise a way as possible. If you want to be successful at something, you first have to make the affirmative decision to do so.

Let me explain the subtitle. *You Ain't Dead Yet* has become a tag line for me. It is often referred to as the New Orleans mouse story. The story is told during my inspirational presentations to provide necessary perspective to attendees.

The story goes back to 1989 when I was working in New Orleans. My wife called me at work around three o'clock one day in a panic. It turns out that a mouse had gotten into the house. Her urgent request was, "Come home now."

I, of course, left immediately and picked up a trap on the way home. When I arrived home, we placed the trap on the floor where she had seen the mouse. All night long she had me checking the trap. No mouse.

The mouse had not come out of hiding by the time I left for work the next day. I did not think about it again until my wife called work at around the same time as the day before. She was practically unintelligible on the phone. It turns out that the mouse was caught in the sticky glue trap (go figure) and it was squeaking. Her urgent instruction was the same as the previous day, "Come home now."

When I arrived home, I offered to throw out the mouse with the trap. She had other plans. She had gotten a shovel from the basement and instructed me to, as humanely as possible, if that even is possible, put the mouse out of its misery. For those animal lovers out there, be patient, this story has a happy ending.

So there I was, on the side of the house, exposed to the street, with a mouse in a sticky glue trap, with a shovel, wearing a new suit and new shoes deciding how to euphonize a mouse as compassionately as I could. So I put the mouse and trap onto the ground and used the shovel to gently, but firmly, "tap" the mouse. When I assessed the situation, I noticed the mouse was still moving, unless it was the breeze that was making the fur move. So I tried again. The fur was still moving. So I tapped it again.

It then occurred to me how ridiculous I looked. At the same time, I felt the presence of someone staring at me. I looked to my left across the street and my eyes locked with a very old lady sitting on a rocking chair on her front porch. After a short, understanding exchange between our eyes, she said something that I will never forget:

"If it ain't dead yet, it ain't gonna die."

Over the years, I have come to think of this exchange. What it means to me is that, whatever happens in your life, you need to realize that "you ain't dead yet." So long as you are living, you still have the ability to live life and succeed. That is a central theme of this book.

Taking into account the pearl of wisdom I learned from my neighbor that day, I went ahead and found a way to set the stunned, but still live, mouse free, albeit far away from my house.

The blazing sun on the cover of the book symbolizes so many things: life, light, vision, energy, intensity, awareness, positivity, integrity, faith, a higher power, a new beginning, rebirth, renewal, enlightenment and so much more. I hope this book truly signifies a new day for the reader.

The sun coming up is the end of the darkness. If you have had prior failures, disappointments, or a traumatic life-changing condition, it is time to decide to end your darkness starting today. The sun rising each and every day is a continual reminder that *you ain't dead yet.*

Getting back to the book, there are no *shoulds, coulds* or *maybe.* What distinguishes the *Decide Success* process is that I actually let you know, tell you, dictate to you, spell out to you, order you, and even command you to do what I propose. If you want options, go somewhere else. I am advocating a specific, disciplined approach. *Decide Success.* In the book, *The Road Less Traveled,* M. Scott Peck describes laziness as evil. I may not go that far, but what I advocate is truly the opposite of laziness. He writes, "Life is a series of problems. Do we want to moan about them or solve them? Do we want to teach our children to solve them? It is in the whole process of meeting and solving problems that life has its meaning. They create our courage and our wisdom."

As the ads say, "Just do it." Don't give yourself a choice. Turn off the doubting Thomas in you. Silence the negative voice in your head. Make the decision to succeed. Decide to succeed. *Decide Success.*

This book should be fun to read. It certainly was fun to write. Be forewarned, I have written some sections purposely in an interactive or conversational format to make you think instead of just read. I'm not going to hit you over the head with the point to every story. You must do some work. Actively read and, when necessary, let the story sink in. I like to say, let it percolate. You may get it while taking a shower tomorrow morning. That is often what happens to me when I am trying to get my head around a difficult, challenging problem.

Decide Success is chock-full of stories and life lessons. A lot of what we're going to do in this book is to look at things in perspective. A different perspective. Often, a very different perspective.

Decide Success! Well, here we go!

PART 1

THE MAPPING PHASE

Chapter 1
Conducting an Assessment

"I don't look to jump over seven-foot bars: I look around for one-foot bars I can step over."

—Warren Buffett

MAPPING PHASE
(1) Conduct an extensive assessment focusing upon interests, abilities, talents, strengths and weaknesses.

Let's jump right into it. We are solving a problem, concern, issue, obstacle, or challenge: you are not as successful in some aspect of your life as you want to be. Otherwise, you would not be reading this book. As with any problem, the first thing you do is gather the facts. At work, you would conduct an investigation to assess the situation. This is not rocket science.

Here is a fun example. I have been involved in a few scavenger hunts both as a child and as an adult. Once you receive a list of items or clues, you are timed in your pursuit of these items, or provided an end time to appear with as many as you can find. Examples are a penny of a certain year, a newspaper from ten days ago, or a picture with a complete stranger living in another state.

The teams that are most successful don't go-go-go, rush or panic. They plan. As everyone else immediately speeds away from the starting point, the winners almost invariably stop, think and *assess*. They determine what the team has in terms of resources, weaknesses (one automobile, one game sheet, two participants who can't drive, and so on), talents, abilities, and strengths.

So the first success principle in making *You* more successful is to conduct an honest assessment of *yourself*. The same can be said if you are assessing your organization. The key word is honest. Take inventory and be as objective as you can be. At the very least, address these six areas:

1.   Discover your unique talents.
2.   Recognize your natural abilities.
3.   Identify areas of intelligence.
4.   Explore your interests.
5.   Describe yourself today.
6.   Play to your strengths.

Be Aware of Weaknesses

This is not to be confused with "beware of weaknesses." Weaknesses are nothing to be ashamed of. Everyone has them. It is important to recognize or be aware of them and acknowledge them, as opposed to denying or ignoring them. You should never stick your head in the sand. I don't know where that expression comes from, but I don't see why anyone would want to stick his or her head in sand. The rest of you would be fully exposed. I guess that is the point. In most cases, you can be successful without ever addressing your weaknesses.

I have great difficulty learning and speaking foreign languages, other than a few popular phrases; that is one of my weaknesses. I have managed to be successful without needing to address this weakness. My career, life, and interests do not require that I become fluent in any foreign language. You need to recognize that, if you choose a life path that involves an area in which you are weak, you will have a bigger challenge to succeed, or you will have to lower your standard of how you define success.

By way of example, in the movie *Rudy*, a boy from Northern Indiana defined success as playing on the Notre Dame College football team during their heyday. The movie is emotionally moving because of Rudy's ability to succeed despite the odds against him and his physical weaknesses. Everyone has weaknesses or, at the very least, things that we don't do well.

Weaknesses can be an outcome of a life-changing condition. For me, my Parkinson's has limited my ability to play many sports. I recognize these additional weaknesses. Although I am aware of them, I choose not to focus on what I can't do, but, instead, I focus upon what I can do.

Exercise 1-a:

List your weaknesses. Do not be ashamed, we all have them. Be honest. Some may surprise even you. Some people call them opportunities or challenges. I prefer weaknesses. Always tell it like it is.

Discover Your Unique Talents and Natural Abilities

Every human being has a unique combination and level of talents and abilities. That's wonderful. No two people are alike. You are that special. In order to begin the process of enhancing and accelerating success, an honest evaluation of your talents and abilities is necessary. For whatever reason, possibly age, time, or illness, your talents and abilities may diminish. Therefore, this becomes an area of continual re-assessment.

For example, some people have a high degree of natural talent and ability in the areas of art, music, sports, video games, writing, or entertaining. This is not to say that someone cannot be successful in an area in which they don't possess natural talent. In fact, the premise that you can be more successful is the basis of this book.

However, by honestly identifying your unique talents and abilities, you can go into your life pursuits with your eyes open to the task ahead of you. Consider again the movie, *Rudy*. He defined success as playing at least one down in any game for the football team. If his expectation of success was to be the starting quarterback, a star player, or even just an occasional starter, it is extremely unlikely that any success principles in the world would have worked.

Having exceptional natural talent or ability in a particular area can be both a blessing and a burden. People sometimes say, "All that talent, what a waste." When someone demonstrates real natural talent, yet chooses to pursue another path, other people may feel a sense of disappointment as if that person had a responsibility to use the talents and abilities.

God has provided each of us with unique talents and natural abilities that we may have the obligation to use to the fullest extent possible. Maybe we do have that responsibility; maybe we don't. If we do, then others may think less of us when we choose not to maximize the use of our natural abilities. By the way, this realization is an example of "awareness" that will be discussed later in the book.

The issue comes to the forefront when people are envious or jealous of the talent or ability, and wish that they had the choice whether to use or squander it. On the flip side, one of the greatest compliments one can bestow on another is to say that that person made the most of their limited ability or talent.

Interestingly, it is not as much a compliment to say that a person with exceptional natural talent or ability used his or her talent to the fullest than it is to say that someone with limited talent did. It is almost a "nothing comment," an afterthought. "Well, they had so much natural talent that the cards were stacked in their favor. Who would not have succeeded with all that talent?"

It actually takes the same amount of commitment and discipline for those with limited natural ability as it does for those with an extraordinary amount of natural ability to make the most of their gifts. In fact, talented people may require more commitment and discipline to succeed. They are often competing on a bigger stage.

I'll give you an example. When I was in high school, I was on a soccer team as a junior. My school had the number one team in New York state—a great team. I never even got any playing time, but I stuck with it and I was there every practice and every game. In my junior year, the two middle schools were playing each other. My younger brother was on one of the teams.

The coach called me over to sit next to him during the game. I didn't think the coach even knew my name, even after two years on the team, because I really was pretty far down the chart. He said, "Tell me about your brother." So, I guess that this was my only entrée to the upper echelon of the coaching staff. My brother scored three unassisted goals and his team won 3-2. He was very talented. I was so proud.

The first day of practice the next year, the coach let me know that my brother was likely to start as a sophomore when I was a senior, which would have been a lot of fun for him. So, my senior year comes and it's Labor Day and there are two practices a day from 9 a.m. to noon and from 1 to 4 p.m.

That day, when we finished the morning session, "These are tough practices," my brother said, "I'm calling mom. I'm going home." I said, "You don't have time. We have practice again at one and you can't miss any practices." He said, "No, you don't understand. I'm going home. I'm done." He never played organized soccer again in his life. This is an example of not making the most of your ability. I'm toiling away every day at practice. I'm not playing any, but I'm sticking it out. I wish I had his ability.

That is not how it worked out. No matter how much I practiced, I would never have his ability. He had the ability and didn't want to stick it out. I chose to do the most with my ability.

This book is all about helping you to make the most out of what you have.

Here is another example. Growing up, my friends and I used to play softball and I really enjoyed it. I got serious about it when I lived in Houston. I was on the state championship team for young lawyers as a shortstop. I played every day. Sometimes I would play four or five games in one day.

Although my brother, as I mentioned, has more natural athletic ability than I have in all sports, I eventually became a better softball player than he is. I certainly followed the twelve *Decide Success* principles in this book. I actually decided that I wanted to succeed at softball and then made it happen.

Let me emphasize the point about abilities. What movie can you think of where someone or a group of people tried as hard as they could even though they didn't have much ability? There are dozens: *Miracle on Ice, Rocky, Braveheart, Gladiator,* and *Remember the Titans.* I could list many others. The underdog story is prevalent. That is the message that comes through when somebody with little ability makes the most of what they have. In this type of movie, people without much natural ability do exceptional things.

Exercise 1-b:

What natural talents/abilities have you recognized in yourself? □

Exercise 1-c:

What natural talents/abilities have you recognized in the people in your organization? What about your organization as a collective unit?

Identify Areas of Intelligence

Similar to talents and abilities, each individual is born with a certain level of intelligence. This is not to say that through education, experience, research, and reading one cannot increase his or her knowledge level, but basic, natural intelligence remains at the same level. Math comes easily to some and others have a very difficult time with it.

No matter how much knowledge one attains, someone who does not "get math" will not somehow magically "get it." As I have said, this does not preclude success, but it is something that needs to be recognized before we choose our life journey and life's destination. This realization also has bearing throughout our lives as we pick and choose the areas in which we decide to be successful.

Exercise 1-d:

Identify subjects or areas in which you have natural intelligence.

Explore Your Interests

Now the fun starts. Exploring your interests. The key word is *your*. There are no right or wrong interests. They are personal to you. They may not make practical sense or may be perceived by others to be a waste of time. However, no one has a vote in this except you.

What do you really *enjoy* doing? What do you *love* to do? I mean really *love to do*. Really enjoy. It is amazing how many people have no answer to this fundamental question. They say, "I never thought about it." What an amazing response.

There are no wrong answers, of course, as long as you don't act on ones that hurt others. But you have to spend time to look deep inside yourself. Be introspective. Every response is as unique as the individual responding.

Here's how I would answer this question. My immediate answer is: I love sports, music, good food, and people. Delving more deeply, I love accomplishing something that I am proud of. I love teaching. I love being on the just side of a situation or issue. I enjoy variety. I enjoy juggling many issues, but also focusing all my energy on a challenging issue. I really like bringing humor into people's lives. I enjoy being with fun loving, positive, energetic people. I love to inspire others. Finally, while some people desperately avoid the spotlight, I like being the center of attention.

You would think the answer would change over the years, as we grow older and mature. I would venture to guess that, in reality, most people's responses would be surprisingly similar no matter what age they are. They may have tried more things so they are better able to identify more specifics, but their general areas of interest remain quite similar. I have always loved sports, competition, success, teaching, justice, laughing, variety, staying active, music, and people. And I still do. The older I get, the more things that I discover things that I love to do, but they do tend to follow the same general themes.

Think of people you know who do what they love. As they say, it is not a job if you are doing what you love to do. I know someone who takes apart Corvettes, engines and all, and then puts them back together again. It was pure bliss for him. If I had to do this, it would have been absolute work.

I live in Kentucky, the horse capital of the world. Those who invest in Thoroughbreds typically don't expect to make any money. It is an expensive hobby. Most hobbies don't eat. But it's pure bliss for them. I would be watching every dollar and worrying constantly.

Success You Truly Desire

How do you know that the interests you have are really *yours*? Interesting question. Your first reaction may be, "Of course they are; I've done them all my life." But how do we know that our interests are truly *ours* and not us trying to live up to someone else's expectations, gain the approval of a particular person or other people, or even reacting to a childhood trauma?

An experience that comes to mind is "est" or Erhard Seminars Training, something in which I participated in 1980 or thereabouts. You might have seen the movie parody *Semi-Tough* where the character played by Burt Reynolds tries to impress a girl by attending an est training (to circumvent the lack of bathroom breaks, he straps on a contraption that allows him to urinate into a bottle strapped to his leg).

The horror stories are true: no outside communication for the entire weekend, sitting for long periods, and rare bathroom breaks. However, the messages are insightful: wake up; take off your blinders; you are a robot reacting every day to what others did to you or drummed into your head in the past; open your eyes, choose your own destiny; break the spell you are under; don't be controlled by some unseen force or bad memory; and decide for yourself. Once you get it, it is both depressing and exhilarating.

Depressing because you recognize that you've wasted so much time and energy on programmed actions, yet it is exhilarating to be on the road to freedom. Much more needs to be done in most cases, but the insights are invaluable. Virtually everyone at the est seminar tied a traumatic childhood experience to either his or her *chosen* profession or the type of spouse they *chose*.

I had another experience with a similar awakening. In the mid-1980s, I discovered the work of John Bradshaw. He had written several books, including *Healing the Shame that Binds You* and *Reclaiming and Championing your Inner Child*. He talked about how difficult it is to change a family system. It was the first time I heard the word *co-dependency*.

Bradshaw described how each member of a family is pigeon-holed or assigned a role. If one family member attempts to redefine himself or herself, the remainder of the family will do all they can to push that member back into his or her role. They may not even know that they are doing it.

This explains, to some degree, what happens during the holidays when families who live far apart get together. The old roles creep in and you find yourself doing things and acting like you used to, regressing to your assigned role.

I had a third similar experience. I recently went on a "New Warrior Weekend" and, although I am bound by an obligation to not share the details, it involved a significant amount of introspection and role-playing. Men looked deep inside themselves to identify events and people who have some invisible control over their present day actions. Once the trauma or relationship is illuminated, the journey to freedom can commence.

Once this work is started (and it is work, very difficult work, which one never actually finishes), interesting things happen. Often a person who was a lifelong hunter or played a certain sport or had a particular hobby may realize that they really did not enjoy this activity. Once they've had this awakening, they can replace those activities with what they truly enjoy and love to do.

These three widely different approaches focused on the same result.

Exercise 1-e:

What are your true interests? What do you *love* to do?☐ ☐ ☐

Describe Yourself Today

So, honestly look at yourself in as an objective a way as you possibly can. Are you happy? What a loaded question that is. It is the age-old universal question. Some of us never think about this. Others never stop.

Am I happy in what way? What facet of my life? What about my profession? Do I like my job-position-work-salary-bonus? How is my marriage or committed relationship? Would I like a better house? Boat? Country club?   What are your questions?

M. Scott Peck writes about assessment by advocating "a life of continuous and never-ending stringent self-examination" and "a life of willingness to be personally challenged." In *The Road Less Traveled.*

I remember in high school that I was stereotyped into a certain role: a nerd. Probably well deserved, but I did not feel like it was the true me. Then I had the opportunity to attend an overnight camp for the entire summer. No one knew anyone else. No preconceived notions. We all could be as we were, or should I say, how we wanted to be.

I was fourteen and suddenly had no past. None of us did. I was as fun loving, kind, and giving as I could be. A good friend to all. Once I got comfortable with my new personality, I was confident enough to be "myself" or my new self back home.

Interestingly, many human resources departments use the PI or predictive index in hiring. The index asks that you first identify characteristics that you believe describe you, and then to list characteristics that you believe others would attribute to you. That's exactly what I am talking about. How can these two lists be different? But they often are. Sometimes they are completely different, even opposite.

Next ask yourself what you dislike doing. You do need to consider this, but don't get bogged down in it or get some measure of comfort from the sympathy of others. The "woe is me" syndrome is paralyzing. Finding out what you dislike can be helpful, if you use it as a motivator to avoid doing those things again.

Fortunately, there are not many things I dislike doing, and even fewer things that I hate doing. I hate being stuck in traffic and driving during thunderstorms. I hate spending extended periods of time in windowless rooms. I dislike many of the opposites of what I love or enjoy doing. I really don't like negative people or complainers; they suck the life and energy out of me.

Exercise 1-f:

Describe yourself today.

Play to Your Strengths

How can we play to our strengths? This is critically important. We first need to identify in what areas we are strong. It is unfortunate that we are often not sent this message.

I'll give you an example. If your son came home from school with an A in math, three Bs and a C, you would naturally get a tutor for the C to shore up the weakness. I don't disagree with that. But think about summer camp and, let's say your son is good in basketball, but terrible in soccer; you wouldn't send him to a soccer camp because he needs to shore up his weakness, would you?

You would send him to a basketball camp, something that accentuates the natural talent and ability he has. So my corollary is to get him a tutor, not just for the C, but get him a tutor for the A, so that he can rise to that next level and maybe become a math professor or do something special in the math field.

I have already mentioned the movie *Rudy*. Let me tell you more about it. Think about the movie story line. It is the story of a Northern Indiana boy who was a marginal high school football player, of below-average size, with even more marginal grades, who decided to apply to attend Notre Dame University, a prestigious academic institution, and find a way to get on the football team during their heyday. Impossible.

It is an inspiring movie and exemplifies all the *Decide Success* principles contained in this book. Rudy was truly an underdog, to the point that many men tear up when Rudy is put into the game at the end of the movie, and tens of thousands of fans chant his name. However, I do want to point out what an incredibly difficult road he chose.

His dream was not in line with his abilities or, as it turns out, with his natural intelligence. I do not mean that people should not dream or go after their dreams, but if you choose a path not in line with your abilities, just be aware of the tremendous task ahead of you.

In Rudy's case, had he been an incredibly gifted athlete who was of great size and who was naturally intelligent, the dream of playing football at Notre Dame would, in fact, require very little effort. During one scene, the head coach tells another player that if he had half the heart that Rudy had, he could be an All-American. The other player had talent, but no idea about how to succeed.

The true outcome in *Rudy* is not lost on me, Rudy ended up with a degree from an excellent academic institution that he would not have obtained had he not had the dream of playing football for Notre Dame. I'm just saying that he chose an incredibly difficult path. As long as you do this with your eyes open, more power to you.

I'll use Tiger Woods as an example of someone with extraordinary talent who took it to the next level. He's got great talent in golf, but he still had to work at it; he still had to put in all the effort; he still had to do all the other things necessary to succeed. The reality is that he could succeed at a higher level than I could ever achieve in golf because he has the natural talent, ability, and intelligence. As I have said, just as it is compliment to say that one has made the most of their natural ability, it is one of the harshest criticisms to say that someone wasted their God-given ability or talent.

So, it's better to swim downstream, than upstream and it's better to run downhill than uphill. Once you have identified your natural talents, abilities, and intelligence, if you focus on your interests and play to your strengths, you can be wildly successful.

It doesn't mean that you give up on your dream. If your dream is to do something for which you don't have a natural ability, you should still go for it, but realize that it's going to be a tougher road than if you played to your strengths and went with what comes naturally.

My point is that you can achieve success going with your abilities and intelligence or going against them; just be aware of the amount of added effort required to commit to a definition of success that is not aligned with your abilities, talent, and natural intelligence.

Exercise 1-g:

List your strengths.☐

Who Do You Ask?

Asking friends to help you with your self-assessment brings up a whole range of issues that must be recognized and taken into account. It is risky for any friend to tell the truth even when it is requested with, as we lawyers would say, absolute immunity. What is said can never be taken back. You cannot strike it from the record or direct the jury to disregard that last remark. It is out there.

My thought is that casual or recent friends will likely not take the risk and will provide useless, if not misleading, feedback. You may receive inaccurate information, what they think you want to hear. This can do more damage than good by reinforcing inaccurate assessments. So I would not recommend asking your "friends."

The only friends to approach are ones with whom you have survived many life experiences and who are willing to risk telling you the truth. Limit this to your closest friends with whom you have history. Value this feedback and discount others who tell you what they think you want to hear.

Why is Simon Cowell, formerly of *American Idol* fame, so popular? He is popular because he is brutally honest. The way most of us would love to be. He got rich doing it. You may enrich a few of your relationships and end many others if you try this. Honesty is a gift rarely risked.

Consider Playing to Your Strengths

So, what do you do with this self-reflection information? Decide. Do you want to swim upstream, run uphill, or swim with the current, travel downhill? Do you use your God-given talents to the best of your ability? Or try to do things that you are not naturally good at and struggle with?

No value judgment, just an observation. Now that you know more about yourself (and please don't shortchange yourself with this introspective process), you have established the foundation for the entire thought process.

If we can get beyond what we were programmed to do caused by some kind of experience, tragic or otherwise (easier said than done), we can delve deep into our soul and reflect on what we truly enjoy...what we love to do. Please note that this can be done at *any* stage of life. There are no age limits. Grandma Moses did not pick up a paintbrush until late in life.

This discussion brings to mind the Serenity Prayer, "Grant me the serenity to accept the things I cannot change, the courage to change the things I can, and the wisdom to know the difference."

Afford a Brick

For me, the first time I can remember doing a honest self-assessment (though, of course, I did not label it that way) was when I was about fifteen years old sitting in the garage of the family home on Long Island. I was looking at the back of the garage and thought to myself, "I cannot even afford one of those bricks. How am I going to afford a whole house?"

I took stock. Decent athlete, but I'm not going to make a living out of it. I do not want to be a doctor. I can't imagine cutting into a human body and blood makes me queasy. I'm no good at foreign languages, so not going to be in a job that requires fluency in a foreign language, especially not a translator.

I would love to teach, but the money is not exceptional (both of my parents were teachers). Fairness seems to be of the utmost importance to me. I'm never one to back down from a challenge or an argument, for that matter. I seem to be a logical thinker and am able to convince others of my point of view. This sounds like an attorney to me.

So, what do we do if we reflect and decide that we are not happy in one respect or another in our life today?

Is it too late? Remember that *you ain't dead yet*. Not if you have a pulse, your heart is pumping, and your brain is functioning. Alone, or with the help of a professional, take an inventory. The first step often is to keep a journal. Write things down.

Chapter 2
Experiencing Your End-vision

"A man is but the products of his thoughts; what he thinks, he becomes."

—Mohandas Gandhi

"I have a dream that my four little children will one day live in a nation where they will not be judged by the color of their skin, but by the content of their character...I have a dream that one day on the red hills of Georgia, the sons of former slaves and the sons of former slave owners will be able to sit together at the table of brotherhood."

—Martin Luther King, Jr.

MAPPING PHASE
(1) Conduct an extensive assessment focusing upon interests, abilities, talents, strengths and weaknesses.
(2) Experience your own end-vision by actually projecting and engaging all your senses, and then identify the specific necessary steps to make it your reality.

Now that you have done an honest assessment of yourself or your organization and have taken inventory, let's proceed to the *Decide Success* action step number two. Once you know where you are, you need to decide where you want to go.

The second principle is what I call "end-vision," a play on the word "envision." Let's look at a vacation analogy. Most people who go on vacation don't just get in the car and start driving. They don't walk up to the first ticket counter in the airport and ask for a ticket on the next flight.

Most people on vacation know where they're going and have planned it out. The same thing should be true with your life. In fact, I would venture to guess that most people put more planning into their family vacation than into their future.

You don't have to know what the vision is right away, but at some point you have to say, "What's the vision?" Then you need to keep the end-vision in mind. What you do is break it down. Once you decide what the end-vision is, you need to plan step by step how to reach it. My end-visions have been quite different over my lifetime, from successfully graduating from school to being successful in my profession to being successful in my personal life.

How do you find your end-vision? What is success to you?

Success is definitely a concept that changes over your lifetime. From sitting to crawling to taking your first steps, the definition of success is constantly evolving. This does not mean you should sell yourself short. You must have "stretch" goals or progress is never made.

Set up a time frame and remind yourself to set aside the time to reassess. Sometimes this is called "tickling." Have you achieved success? Are you on your way? How far along are you? Have you added new ways to measure success? Are adjustments necessary? Is reassessment warranted? Like weighing yourself while on a diet, you should not do this too frequently. Once a month is likely sufficient.

I held a success workshop for inner-city teenagers and asked this question. The insightfulness and clarity of their responses amazed me. Some of them defined success as, "a place to stay for more than a few days at a time, " "a mattress on a bed to sleep on instead of the floor, " "a house, " and "not having to go to sleep hungry." It reminded me of an experience that I had one summer during my college years selling dictionaries door-to-door just south of Houston, Texas. What struck me, slapped me in the face, was how unhappy most of the rich people seemed and how much happier poor people seemed. Invariably, when I knocked on the door in the wealthy areas of town, I was greeted with a scowl. You could see the unhappiness in their faces. Sometimes there was a false smile at first, to be followed by what was natural for them, a pained expression. Now, I was not a pushy salesperson, so a polite "not interested" was always accepted. And most of the time, I could sense that I was not interrupting something urgent.

By contrast, the overall impression I had in the poorer areas was genuine comfort and graciousness. Of course, nothing is absolute; there were exceptions, but the old adage that money does not buy happiness rang true. I made a promise to myself that I have always kept. No matter how much money or assets I have, I will appreciate whatever I do have and be happy with it. In fact, there are only two material things that hold any significance for me; both remind me of times when I achieved some measure of success that I will discuss below.

Make-a-Wish

I am the current chair of the Make-A-Wish Foundation, Kentucky chapter, Board of Directors. The mission of the organization is to grant wishes to the entire families of children with life-threatening conditions. I love this organization. Maybe it has to do with my daughter's birth defects and cerebral palsy, but I really can empathize with the families. The parents are facing the possibility of losing a child, something unimaginable. The siblings often do not receive the parental attention that they require. Finally, the child. A life filled so far with doctors, hospitals, shots, and pain. When a child decides upon his or her wish, they are unknowingly engaging in an end-vision. The child, with the help of a wish volunteer, actually imagines themselves and their entire family experiencing the wish. Often it is Disneyworld. The wish child often can experience the enjoyment of being there weeks before the actual trip. And experience some medical improvement—a true end-vision.

End-Vision as a Reward

End-visions come in all shapes and sizes. Here is another of mine. Both of my parents were teachers, and with three children in four years, they helped with college as best they could. Financially, I made it through undergraduate and law school, an Ivy League one at that, by the skin of my teeth. I had run out of money, loan capacity and maxed out all my credit cards on my graduation day. To this day, I could not tell you how I did it.

I barely made expenses several times and several things had to fall into place just right for me to make it through school. I did have to make sacrifices. One was to not have a car in high school and almost all of my college years. Even when I did have a car, it truly was a beater.

During my first year at Cornell Law in Ithaca, New York, where it is cold in the fall, winter, and spring (the entire time school was in session), I would fall asleep under several blankets to minimize the expense of fuel oil and think of buying my dream car if I made it through.

What does every red-blooded American male want?
A car, of course. My dream was to own a Corvette. Not just any old Corvette, I wanted to have a red Corvette. I dreamed of buying a convertible with a black interior. The car had to be a six-speed stick shift. As described in the Prince song, I wanted my own *little red corvette*.

I could close my eyes and feel the vibration of the engine while I sat in the driver's seat of the car. I could smell the leather seats and hear the roar of the engine as I eased on the gas pedal and put it in gear. I could see trees go by in a blur and feel the wind going through my hair. A true end-vision.

Showing off the ability to own a nice car is not my definition of success. However, when it is a symbol or a reminder to yourself of a successful accomplishment, it represents success to you in a very personal way. If your parents are wealthy and give you an expensive car on your sixteenth birthday and you have not earned it, it has nothing to do with success. Success comes from earning what you have. In fact, what is often lost along the way is to enjoy the moment, enjoy the journey. Keep your eye on the prize, but don't get so focused that you miss out on life.

End-Vision to Prove You Can

Another example of end-vision for me was when I decided to cut down the trees myself on my five-acre lot to clear space for a house and driveway. I was forced to give up softball and tennis due to developing Parkinson's disease and wanted to prove to myself that Parkinson's could not prevent me, at forty-six years old, from doing something physically exhausting. My end-vision was a perfectly cleared footprint for my house. I could see myself in the house, hear the sounds of the wildlife and smell the trees.

So, I bought a cheap chainsaw and returned it. Bought another discount one and returned it. Then bought a Stihl chainsaw and loved it. I had some friends teach me how to use it safely, if that is possible, and got started.

It took me nine months of working nearly every weekend to take down and cut up at least fifty trees. Success. Had some scary moments along the way, but what true success does not have a few of those? What came to mind several times was the film *Monty Python's Holy Grail* when "Sir Robin ran away." I definitely ran away a few times. Some trees have a mind of their own. Sometimes the saw blade all of a sudden was part of the tree and wouldn't budge.

In the end, the sense of accomplishment and success was exhilarating. But I also enjoyed every second along the way. From the one time that my sixteen-year-old son "helped" me by moving broken branches as slowly as any human being could possibly move them, to sitting on a stump drinking an ice-cold beer when I was finished for the day, I enjoyed it all.

I experienced the end-vision of a perfectly cleared lot a good year before it was accomplished. I was there. Standing in the middle of an overgrown mess of trees and underbrush, I could envision exactly what the lot would look like. I felt what it would feel like to look out of the back windows of my house into the wooded forest. I could smell the crisp air. I could see the light shining through the thinned-out trees.

I once heard that Michelangelo described his David sculpture as already existing inside the marble; his job was to chip away the excess. Not to in any way compare myself to Michelangelo, but I felt the same way as I selected which trees to clear. The footprint for the house presented itself within the context of not having to sacrifice even one exceptional tree. A true end-vision.

End-Vision in a Profession

I already touched upon my revelation at sixteen that I was concerned about my future ability to support myself, let alone a family. I remember in tenth grade standing in my garage. I don't know why this was such a watershed moment for me, but I looked at the house we lived in and thought, "I couldn't afford one of these bricks. How am I going to support a family someday?" I knew I wasn't doing great in school, and that I would have to make some changes, because I wanted to have nice things. I'm not ashamed to say this. I also wanted to be able to support a family.

So, what I did was I decided I wanted to be an attorney. In fact, I decided to be a success as a lawyer. Why did I decide that? Because I evaluated myself (step one: assessment) and said, "All right, what do I like to do?"

Fairness is extremely important to me. My parents will tell you I strenuously discussed many things with them when I was in high school; in other words, I argued a lot. Often beyond what was reasonable. I spent most of my childhood up in my room after being sent there as punishment. Of course, I did not have an Xbox, computer, cell phone, DVD player, or even a TV in my bedroom, so it truly was a punishment.

But my decision to become an attorney was not all about earning potential. If I thought something was unfair, I would speak up, whether it was the imposition of a punishment on me, my brother, sister, whatever. I was overboard on that, no question about it. Fairness is important to me. I'm competitive. I think that I can speak well. No surprise here, I like to be the center of attention.

So, these characteristics fit the job of an attorney. I envisioned myself as an attorney. Although I love inspirational speaking, writing, and teaching, my first love is the law. I still practice law, but am now able to pick and choose what cases I want to take on and that goes back to my compulsion to address unfairness.

I have combined my practice with my Parkinson's. I provide advice and representation to employers who want to do the right thing and comply with the law, and employees with a life-changing condition who are not treated properly (not with the same company, of course). In fact, I recently tried a lawsuit that was described as "unwinnable." You will have to wait for Chapter 5 to find out more.

Think about the word *envision*. Think of it as *end-vision*. I pictured myself in court years before I set foot in a courthouse. I felt what it was like to argue a point before the court. I experienced the exhilaration of winning a case. I even could taste the rush of a damaging cross-examination. I felt the sense of pride representing a client in court as their attorney—a true end-vision.

To have an "end-vision" is to actually see yourself in the future. You don't just set a goal or have a vision, but you see where you want to be in the future and you can feel it, touch it, taste it, even though it's not there yet.

End-Vision: A Life-Changing Condition

I went through this transformation once I developed Parkinson's. I went back to *Decide Success* action step one and made a re-assessment, an honest re-assessment, of what I wanted to do. First, I found out as much as I could about Parkinson's. Second, I end-visioned having the slowest progressing condition as ever recorded in the annals of modern medicine.

End-Vision: A Dramatic Life Renovation

When you make a change in your life situation, it often has significant ramifications for others. You might change employers, change professions, change a long-term relationship, sell or purchase a business, move to a new location to live, go back to school, change jobs at the same company, whatever. With respect to these types of decisions, conducting an end-vision process is truly beneficial.

Picture yourself after the change—right after, sometime after, or a significant time period after—whatever makes sense. Picture yourself there. Actually feel yourself there. Use your senses. As goofy as it sounds, close your eyes and see if you can smell what it smells like. Taste what it tastes like. Be there. Live it in your mind. Experience it. Reach out and touch it. That is what "end-vision" is.

I recently went through a very dramatic life renovation. In the summer of 2007, I took stock of my life, starting with my marriage of eighteen years. My wife and I had two children who were getting older, sixteen and eleven. For most of our marriage, I believed that something critical was missing. When the family traveled with two other families for a week in April to Florida and work was not a distraction, I realized how far apart we were. How we did not fulfill each other's needs.

I came up with a list of items to use in evaluating my relationship with my significant other. This is what I came up with: appreciation, affirmation, affection, passion, and intimacy. In any relationship, the individuals have a better chance of being fulfilled and the relationship being healthy if they match up in these areas.

For me, I very much need to be appreciated, to hear that I am loved and express the same, to give and receive a lot of affection, have a very passionate life and love life, and be in a relationship with a high degree of openness and intimacy, sharing every thought and feeling. What I recognized was that my wife and I just did not fit. As my daughter later put it, I was a cup holder and my spouse was a juice box; both are fine just the way they are, they just don't fit together.

The "relationship five" focused my thinking and allowed me to clarify in my mind where I was. We tried to save the marriage, but once I finally made the decision that I had to move on, I went through the end-vision process to visualize and experience two years from that date. I knew it would be a stressful and torturous transition and I remember wishing I could fast-forward at least one year.

Here was my end-vision: I would be living in a newly built, modest house on my five-acre lot in the woods. My son, daughter, ex-wife, and parents would accept and understand my decision. Maybe not agree with it, but accept it. That's it. I saw myself there. I could feel it. I knew it was right. I was so much happier. Once I completed the end-vision process, I knew that everyone involved that was important to me, including myself, would be better off, and happier in the long term, when I made the change.

On separate occasions, each of my children asked (begged, pleaded with) me to get back together with their mother. I knew it was not the right thing to do for everyone involved. In fact, the passage of time has shown this to be true. My former wife is happier with her significant other and I am happier with mine. *But*, I was tempted. Had I not gone through the end-vision process and actually experienced what my life would be like, I might have given in. After all, these are my children. I would take a bullet for either of them. But, as adults, we have the obligation of doing what is best, not what is popular or easy.

In addition, on some level, I knew that my former wife did not have it in her to be a good caregiver. She needs someone to take care of her. She now has that. And with my Parkinson's, I will eventually need someone who is strong, a survivor. I now have that. For all these reasons, both consciously and sub-consciously, I knew that I should stay the course. My end-vision gave me the strength and conviction.

Inspirational Speaker

In my most recent end-vision I am someone who speaks to audiences and helps people get through the same issues that I've been through and maybe help them do it a little bit better than I did. My intern asked me, of all the activities that I am involved in, which is the most important to me. I thought about it and decided that helping others become more successful and inspiring others are my main missions. That is what I end-vision.

It is not about fame or money or anything related to me personally. My end-vision is seeing understanding in the eyes of audience members. Feeling the hugs from audience members who have been inspired. That is my end-vision on a regular basis.

Whatever allows me to reach as many people as possible is something that I will do. If I have to publish a book, conduct seminars, market myself, or even become a celebrity to reach as many people as possible, I will do it. The point is that I have no interest in becoming famous for the sake of being famous. If I need to do so to reach as many people as possible, so be it. If I can do so without becoming famous, fine by me.

The Secret: Vision without Steps

The DVD entitled *The Secret* has been discussed and marketed extensively. What I get out of it is that you must envision yourself where you want to be. The DVD states, "If you go to the mailbox expecting there to be bills, there will be. If you go to the mailbox expecting checks made out to you, that's what you will find."

Interesting, but what is missing are the details. The behind-the-scenes work—the steps taken to make this a reality. It doesn't just happen. Maybe it won't happen if you don't envision yourself there, but you also can't spend all of your time envisioning and spend no time making it happen.

Specific Actions: Beyond the Secret

Once I envisioned what I wanted my future to be, I had to make it happen. It is a step-by-step process. For example, When I was a tenth grade student, what were specific, identifiable, and measurable things that I would have to do that day and the next day to end up as an attorney?

When I present the *Decide Success* principles in a workshop or seminar, the interplay is often as follows when I ask the attendees what steps anyone would need to take as a tenth-grader to eventually become a successful attorney.

What did I need to do the next day after having the end-vision? Often the response is, "Go to class." Let's expand on that; what needed to be done? Do you just need to show up in class, sit there, and fall asleep? The response usually was, "Take notes. Listen and learn." And the phrase "get good grades" is sometimes brought up next.

So we have good grades and learn the material, what are the other two things that needed to be done to become an attorney? You need to engage in extracurricular activities to enhance your application to college. That is the third one. The fourth is maybe the most apparent, but often not thought of until the end. College costs money. You need money to go to college so, for me, I had to work after school.

When broken down, we have four tangible things: get good grades, learn, build up extracurricular activities to get into a good school, and earn money. Those are the four specific, practical, measurable things that you could work on every day.

After graduating from high school, you go to college. What needs to be done in college? What are specific, identifiable, and measurable things that need to be done in college? Make money. What else? Need to learn. Learn, what else? Good grades. What else? Resume or application items.

Just so happens that's the same four things, break it down, that's what you need to do in college. You need to keep your eye on the ball, focus on these four things. Now you go to law school and guess what? What do you need? Money, resume; grades, learning.

What about once you take a position as an attorney? You don't have grades any more, or do you? What are performance reviews, but real-world grades? You also still need to learn; you have on-the-job training. They don't teach you how to be a lawyer at law school, they just teach you how to think like a lawyer. And extracurricular activities are really up to the individual, unless you are in a law firm, where you need to make contacts in order to bring in clients, then it's still important.

That's just one example of how you break it down. Plan it out and break it down step by step: specific, tangible, and measurable steps.

Plan Step by Step

What do you need to do today? Tomorrow? Next week? Next month? Next year?

Exercise 2-a:

Write the word "**IMPOSSIBLE**" in bold, capital letters as big as you can on the biggest piece of paper you can find. Color it in. Be as creative as you can be. *Now tear it to shreds. Keep the pieces as a reminder that nothing is impossible.*

- Is it impossible to put a human being on the moon?
- Is it impossible to put your ear to a small piece of metal and hear the voice of someone thousands of miles away?
- Is it impossible to replace a person's bad heart with a good one that used to be in someone else's body?
- Is it impossible for a person with one hand to play baseball in the major leagues?
- Is it impossible for a 5'3" person to play professional basketball in the NBA?
  Is it impossible for a 400,000 pound piece of metal carrying humans to fly through the air and land safely?

Babe Ruth and the Not-so-Famous Rick Ankiel

What could a modern-era ballplayer possibly have in common with the great Babe Ruth, the Sultan of Swat, the Great Bambino? Well, each did what is, if not impossible, close to it. Most people know that Babe Ruth was the Home Run King. What most non-baseball fans are unaware of is that the Great Bambino started out as a pitcher and had 94 career wins. He even threw a shutout in a World Series game for the Boston Red Sox. He was just such a great hitter that the team moved him to the outfield to be an everyday player.

Rick Ankiel ended up in the same place in a very different fashion. In 2000, twenty year-old pitcher Rick Ankiel won eleven games for the St. Louis Cardinals, had a respectable 3.50 earned run average, and struck out 194 batters. What happened to him was painful to watch. In the third inning of a playoff game, he walked four batters and threw five wild pitches. He lost all control of his pitches. In his next start, he was removed in the first inning of that playoff game after throwing twenty pitches, five of which went past the catcher, the first of which sailed over the head of the batter. Finally, Ankiel appeared in a third playoff game facing four hitters, walking two, and throwing two more wild pitches.

Rick Ankiel was finished as a major league ballplayer. Or so we thought. Seven years later at the ripe old age of 27, a ballplayer named Rick Ankiel made his "debut" in the major leagues...as an outfielder.

Impossible or, at least, so it seems. Over the 2007 and 2008 baseball seasons, Rick Ankiel played 167 games (a little more than one full season), had 158 hits including thirty-six home runs and 110 runs batted in. In 2009 and 2010, he made a total of over $5.5 million dollars. Nothing is impossible.

Unsolvable Math Problem Solved

End-visions can occur even when you don't intend to engage in the process. Here is an example of an end-vision based upon being unaware of limits established by others.

I once heard a story that I hope is true. It involved a college graduate student majoring in math who was late to class. He dutifully copied down the two problems on the blackboard upon his late arrival.

When it was time to do the homework problems, he found them very difficult. Being a straight A student, he was in a panic and stayed up all night working on the math problems. Finally, near dawn, he solved the first one.

He ran out of time and, dejectedly, went to the professor's office and slid the homework under his door with a note of apology for being late for class and not solving the second homework problem. He was so depressed and embarrassed that he drew the shades and went to sleep. About 4 p.m. that afternoon, there was an urgent knock on his door. He was surprised to find the chair of the math department at his door.   He had been late to class, submitted an incomplete homework assignment, and slept though class that day. The only thing he could conclude, seeing the chair at his door, was that he was being expelled.

Much to his surprise, the department chair excitedly explained that the student had done the impossible. He had solved what was thought to be an unsolvable math problem that stumped even Einstein. You see, he missed the start of class where the professor informed the class that the problems were impossible to solve. Take the word impossible out of your vocabulary.

Exercise 2-b:

What are your end-visions?
(1)
(2)
(3)

Exercise 2-c:

For each end-vision, identify specific necessary actions to make it your reality.☐

End-vision #1 actions:

End-vision #2 actions:

End-vision #3 actions:

PART 2

THE
WORK
PHASE

Chapter 3
Putting Forth Your Best Effort

"Action is no less necessary than thought to the instinctive tendencies of the human frame."

—Mohandas Ghandi

MAPPING PHASE
(1) Conduct an extensive assessment focusing upon interests, abilities, talents, strengths and weaknesses.
(2) Experience your own end-vision by actually projecting and engaging all your senses, and then identify the specific necessary steps to make it your reality.
WORK PHASE
(3) Put forth your absolute best effort—be resilient.

Best Effort: Door-to-door Sales

Here is the first example of putting out your absolute best effort. I sold books in Houston, Texas, door to door during the summer, when it was hot, real hot. Talk about exhausting, physically and mentally. I knew that at each house, the chance of rejection was about 95 percent. It was the hardest thing I've ever done in my life, before or since, hands down, no question about it. Walking up to each door, knowing that nineteen times out of twenty the door would be slammed in my face. Then I would have to go to the next door. The hours were incredible and the heat was awful. Knocking on doors from 7:30 a.m. to

9:30 at night, six days a week. There were even sales meetings on Sunday mornings. No rest for the weary.

A lot of the people who signed up became burned out and gave up. As physically, mentally, and emotionally draining as it was, and it was all of that and more, I made the commitment to myself to stick it out. To be resilient. Not only did this summer job bring financial rewards, but it also bolstered my self-confidence, self-image and self-esteem.

Nothing I have ever done in my life has been as difficult as this job. It took my absolute best effort to get through the summer. I was able to create a new standard for how I defined hard work.

Championship: A True Team Effort

Here is an article written as a tribute to my son that exemplifies effort and hard work:

A Tribute to the Other Trinity State Champion Football Players

There are more players on Trinity High's football team than possible jersey numbers. Realistically, only sixty to seventy players can get into a game leaving at least fifty players on the sideline.

My son loves to play football. As a freshman, with over 100 on the roster, he had difficulty getting playing time. He knew this year it would be even more difficult to get into a game. Why did he still make the tremendous sacrifice and time commitment to be a Trinity football player? The simple answer is, my son loves Trinity football.

Starting in January, he went to conditioning and weight training. When he tells Coach Maddox stories, you can tell what a positive influence the man is in my son's life In fact, my son has a football card from when Maddox was a coach at University of Louisville. From January to June, he never missed a session. Sounds like not many of the boys did.

My son comes from a Red Sox family. We scheduled a trip with my father to see the Red Sox play in Phoenix, but it would have meant that my son would miss two sessions. In addition, two weeklong summer trips were also planned, one out of the country and the other a family reunion. I even discussed whether I could get him excused with principal of the school. He suggested that my son write a note to the head coach. I went so far as to draft the note myself. My son never even considered it. His response was simply, "You don't know the Trinity way, Dad.

From July to December, he never missed a conditioning session, practice, or game. Not many did. To watch the starters during the game give pointers to the others is a marvelous tribute to the legacy of Coach Beatty and the Trinity football program. To think about the compensation paid to each of the coaches, if any at all, in relation to the commitment and effort put in, is mind boggling.

It is hard to see the contribution the others make when they spend all their time during the games on the sidelines. There are no spectators at practice when the effort made by the others makes the team better and better. He complained about, but loved, as a lineman, carrying the ball during practice and getting destroyed by the starting defense. Many bruises demonstrate his commitment.

Championship week my son was so nervous he had a hard time sleeping. All he wanted for Christmas was "the ring." In quiet moments, he wondered whether they would win the rematch against their rival St. Xavier. My response was five words, "Have faith in Coach Beatty." Without hesitation, he said, "We do."

I never doubted that Trinity would win that game. Even when it looked unlikely, I knew that the conditioning all the boys committed themselves to, all those hours, sacrifices made, missed vacations, sweat and effort would be factors, and in the end they were. My son has every right to call himself a state football champion. So do all the others.

A Proud Trinity Dad

My son understands effort and hard work. Football has taught him that. His junior year, when he came to me frustrated at getting no playing time, the only response that I could come up with was, "You're on the football team to stay in good physical shape, be a part of a team, and to include it in your college applications. Think of playing time as a bonus and be proud of the fact that your team is so good that you can't get any playing time." It might have been small consolation, but it kept him going. It allowed him to continue to put out his best effort and work hard.

What happens when you put out your best effort and work hard? You prove something to yourself about yourself. You build self-confidence. Key word: *self*. Have you ever known someone in whom you have more confidence than they do themselves? We all do. Hard work improves self-esteem, self-confidence, and self-image.

Even if you don't meet your goals, if you can look yourself in the mirror and say that you did the best; gave it 100 percent; left it all out there on the field, there was nothing else you could have done, no additional effort could have been made—then you have enhanced your self-confidence.

The interesting thing about effort and hard work is you need no talent or ability to do it. You simply have to make the decision to do it and then do it. *Decide Success.* As Nike would say, "Just do it." It is totally within your power and control, and you need ask no one's permission.

I often get asked why I include this one. Isn't effort and hard work a given? Maybe. It may be common knowledge. But do people really do it? Or do most people get disheartened or make excuses? Rationalize that it's not worth the effort. Is hard work common practice?

Anyone who truly wants to succeed must put in the time, best effort and work, even though those who have tremendous ability or talent may not need to, especially those who have the talent. *Decide Success*. The legacy of doing what rarely or never has been accomplished has to be a motivator to these gifted individuals.

You are Not College Material: Motivation for Best Effort

Here is a almost unbelievable example of how far someone can advance by out-working others and expending a greater effort than everyone else.

My father's parents grew up in New York City in areas inhabited by people who emigrated from Germany and Ireland. To even marry, my grandparents had to overcome a lot. He was Jewish and she was Catholic. They had three children: Rita, and then three years later, Edward, and, seven years after that, John, my dad, who was likely a surprise.

Rita married Ed, a blue-collar skilled laborer. They lived across from Kennedy Airport outside New York City. They were literally across from the airport. When we were visiting, you had to pause any conversation when planes were taking off or landing.

My Aunt Rita had four children, one of whom was my cousin Ed. A guidance counselor told him that he was not college material and needed to learn a trade. Sometimes someone telling you that you can't do something ends up being the strongest motivator to put out your best effort.

Despite this sage advice, Ed was accepted into a program at Northeastern University in Boston that had six months of classes, six months co-op, and so on for five years. One of his co-op assignments was with Exxon and the company ended up hiring him after he graduated.

Thirty years later, Ed Galante was the subject of an article in *Fortune* magazine as one of the two favorites to succeed the CEO of ExxonMobil.

Ed was described in the article as a product of the East Coast whose accent still carries traces of a boyhood in Queens and on the South Shore of Long Island. He ran the Baton Rouge refinery, managed Exxon's Central American and Caribbean operations before serving as the CEO's executive assistant. "Galante ran the executive suite when Raymond (the outgoing CEO) was unavailable, and had to decide when to phone the CEO in the middle of the night."

Ed explained to me one time that he prided himself on how hard he worked at his job. But, he added, when he did not get along with his supervisor, he worked even harder to advance out of the situation.[1]

Beatles Outlier Effort

In his wonderfully insightful book, *Outliers*, Malcolm Gladwell states that it takes a 10,000-hour commitment of time to be successful at anything. Most people assume that the Beatles were just naturally gifted as musicians and songwriters and that they did not have to put out any effort to be superstars.

That may be true, but the surprising part is how the Beatles became an "overnight success." They signed on to perform in Germany for a very ambitious and time-consuming schedule. They were forced to come up with new songs when they ran out of songs created by other musical groups.

They put in the work to be successful. Ten-thousand hours is a lot of hours.

---

[1] Nelson O. Schwartz, "Goodbye, Mr. Exxon: Who will replace the ultimate oil guy?" *Fortune*, September 15, 2003

Albert J. Deluca

My grandfather was the kindest, gentlest, and hardest working man I ever met. I spent one summer with him and my grandmother when I was fourteen years old. He owned a corner grocery, grill, and candy store. I particularly liked the candy store.

I shadowed him that summer while he performed his daily routine. Up at 4 a.m. to make coffee for the shoe factory workers that we sold for twenty-five cents a cup. You could only have it two ways: black or regular (cream and sugar). No espresso, latte, cappuccino, grande, venti, or trenta.

From there, we went back to the store to open it to the early morning crowd. Breakfast on the grill. Pick up some groceries. Start making the lunch special (American Chop Suey was my favorite; don't ask what it is, I have no idea). Serve the lunch crowd. Enjoy a frappe as a reward. Clean up.

At around 2 p.m., my grandmother would relieve us for a couple of hours so we could grab a nap at home. I was worn out. Back to serve the dinner crowd. Close at 9 p.m. Back to bed. Get up at 4 a.m. Do it all over again. Seven days a week. "Funnest" summer I have ever had. Great exposure to a true work ethic from a great man. I am who I am today, in no small part, because of him.

Exercise 3:

Give one or more examples in your life of where you gained self-confidence by putting forth your best effort and working hard.□

Chapter 4
Preparing and Practicing

"By failing to prepare, you are preparing to fail."

—Benjamin Franklin

MAPPING PHASE
(1) Conduct an extensive assessment focusing upon interests, abilities, talents, strengths and weaknesses.
(2) Experience your own end-vision by actually projecting and engaging all your senses, and then identify the specific necessary steps to make it your reality.
WORK PHASE
(3) Put forth your absolute best effort—be resilient.
(4) Prepare and practice until you are ready, then prepare and practice some more—be diligent.

"P" for Perseverance

The fourth of the *Decide Success* principles begins with the letter "P." Perseverance? Persistence? Patience? Those are all good. But I am thinking of a more practical p. *Decide Success* principle number four is: prepare and practice.

Stalking: Interview Preparedness

Let me tell a story of being prepared. When I was interviewing for a job in 1996, I looked on the Internet, Googled the company name, and I found as much as I could about the company.

Stop me here. You may be surprised to learn that the Internet was not widely available in 1996. I had to do it the old-fashioned way. I went to the library. I found and read a profile on the company. I even knew the names of the children of the CEO and how old they were. When I got into the interview, I walked up to him and, to demonstrate how prepared I was, I said, "Nice to meet you, and how are Joey and Paige doing in middle school?"

When I do this presentation at college, I receive many strange looks and comments at this point like, "Did he think you were going to kill his kids?" or "What are you, a stalker?" I obviously didn't walk up to him and say that.

But you know how an interview is when you're nervous and you're trying to think about what to say next, how you look, whether you remembered to button your top button, what does the interviewer think of you, what questions should you ask, why is the interviewer asking you that question, everything like that. Needless to say, with all that going through your mind, sometimes you may not be listening as well as you could. I did enough research and was prepared enough to not have to worry about that.

During the interview, the CEO actually mentioned his son's name, Joey. What if I had responded. "How old is Jimmy?" and he would have had to correct me and say, "My son's name is Joey." An awkward moment at best. That didn't happen. Why didn't it happen? Because I memorized his son's name. I was prepared. I didn't know if I was ever going to need it, but think about that awkward moment that didn't happen.

School is My Job: Class Preparedness

Preparation can often be described as being diligent. When I started law school, my first class was at 8 a.m. It was my contract class. My next class was at 10 a.m. What do you think I did from 9 a.m. to 10 a.m.? Study, right? Do you think that I studied for the class I just took or the one I'm about to go into? Why would I study for the one I just took? I don't have that class again until the next day. The answer is: the class I just had.

Why? To retain what I just learned, rewrite my notes, make associations. I would do the homework for that class that I just took right after the class, because it was fresh in my mind and it made more sense, and I learned more. That is the point of law school, to learn the materials presented.

Most of the other students took a coffee break between classes, but I went right to the library and did the next assignment. Discipline. Diligence. From 10 a.m. to 11 a.m., I had class. From 11 a.m. to 2:30 p.m., besides lunch, what do you think I did? Homework for that class.

This is the tough one; I had class from 2:30 to 3:30. What do you think I did after class? Homework. Sometimes that class wouldn't meet until the next week, which made it more important to do the homework right away, right after class. While everyone else was playing touch football and goofing around, especially if it was a nice day, I studied.

What did I notice my other classmates were doing? Ever hear of pulling all-nighters in law school? They were pulling all-nighters. What happens when you pull an all-nighter? What happens? You don't retain as well. You're tired, you don't always go to class the next day and sometimes you miss class. You have to make it up sometime; after you pull an all-nighter, you have to sleep sometime.

Every day at 5 p.m., I was done. So I could go out to a nice dinner, maybe stay out, have a few drinks, whatever, and be in bed by 10 p.m. and up for the 8 a.m. class. I did it every day. Now, did I have to do that to succeed? I don't know. But once you start doing something, it becomes a habit.

You get disciplined, put in the hard work, prepare, you just do it. *Decide Success.* It had major benefits for me, because at 5 p.m. every day I had a sense of relief; everything was done. I read all the assignments and I retained it better.

So, that's an example of preparation. Everyone can do that, you just do it. There's no magic, no ability, no intelligence, you just do it. *Decide Success.*

What else does preparation do for you? It relieves or at least minimizes stress. At 5 p.m. every school day at law school, I could relax. I did not have homework hanging over my head. I have found that, although a healthy amount of stress can be a great motivator, so can *not* having to experience stress. I find that, with Parkinson's, my health literally depends upon minimizing daily stress.

Study Group: Exam Preparedness

As a follow-up to being prepared for classes as described above, students need to be prepared for exams. In law school, some other students and I formed a study group for exam preparation. Each of us took a subject and presented to the group an outline and an oral presentation with a question-and-answer session.

An interesting thing occurred when we received our exam grades. The group member that presented on a subject received his or her highest grade in that subject class. Makes perfect sense. When you have to teach the subject, sometimes called in business "train the trainer," you have to know the subject in more depth. You prepare in a different way.

Availability of Prior Exams to Prepare

The coolest example of the benefits of preparation is this one. As one of my professors in college was droning on, Management 101, he said, "We're going to have four exams in this class, three during the semester and one as the final. Only three grades count; an average of the three best grades you receive is your grade. Past exams are in the library.

So, how many students do you think blew off the first exam? After all, only three count. What's the other alternative? Prepare seriously for the first three exams. Ace the first three, then you don't have to take the final exam. Then I would have fewer finals and less pressure. I had more time to prepare for the ones I did have to take. I was amazed to see how many blew off the first exam, thinking that one did not count anyway.

And the professor said the previous exams were in the library. I checked it out; there were only twelve out of the 150 students who checked out the exams, who took a look at the previous exams. What do you think happened when I prepared by answering the prior exam questions? I used them as a study guide to prepare for each exam. There was nothing I hadn't seen already. Teachers are lazy; half the questions were the same. I already looked them up; it was like I was handed the exam weeks in advance. Preparing by using the previous exams provided a significant advantage.

NFL Head Coaches: Game Preparedness

When I think of preparation, the extreme seems to be the horror stories of football, especially the coaches. One week (sometimes less) to come up with a game plan to defeat a different team each week for at least a dozen weeks, plus playoffs. Oh yes, there is a bye week during the NFL season where, I'm sure, the coaching staff take a week off and go on vacation. Not.

No wonder Tony Dungy, the coach of the Indianapolis Colts, retired at the age he did. The hours! The meetings! Watching film! Drawing up complicated plays early enough in the week to teach them to eleven men (some with intelligence, some without) plus substitutes, so they all know their assignments! Knowing that winning or losing the game may depend upon one missed assignment. Why do they prepare to this insane degree? Well, because they know that the other guy is. Would it make sense to take a chance and do a half-cocked job at preparing?

ST. Patrick's Football: Sports Preparedness

Even for football at the middle school level, the preparation can be extreme. I was on a staff of eleven coaches for a seventh and eighth grade school team. Eleven coaches. We went away on a retreat before the season with the fifth and sixth grade coaches to get scouting reports on players going into seventh grade. This was for middle school recreational sports. During the season, we watched film of the team we were playing the next weekend. For hours and hours. In slow motion! We watched film of our game, each play individually as many times as players we could see. Unbelievable preparation! But we were prepared each and every week. And it paid off.

Trial Preparedness

Similar to football coaches, trial attorneys depend upon preparation to be successful at trial. The rules of civil procedure provide for extensive information to be exchanged before trial in order for both sides to have the opportunity to be fully prepared. This is called discovery. Whatever you think of the system of justice, the rules give everyone the opportunity to be prepared. In fact, the criminal system provides even more opportunity as the character portrayed by Marisa Tomei points out in *My Cousin Vinny*. Her character tells the character played by Joe Pesci that the prosecutor must turn over his entire file to the defense. Preparation is one vital key to success. You just have to decide to do it. *Decide Success.*

Free Throw Practice

Practice is a significant aspect of preparation. The best example that I can use is practicing free throws. Whatever the situation, the physical attributes don't change. The foul line in every gym in the world is exactly the same distance from the basket. The rim is exactly the same height. The cleared space in front is exactly the same. The basketball is the same size. The opening for the basket is exactly the same.

Why is it then that someone may make a higher percentage of free throws all alone in the gym than during a real game? What about in the last few seconds of a close game? Nerves. Some thrive on them. Some break under them. One of the few things that can be done to improve your odds of making those critical free throws is to practice, practice, practice. Make it so second nature, so automatic, so familiar that no game situation can rattle you from your routine.

Everything I've talked about up to this point can be done by anyone. If you just commit to do it, you can do it, and, without a doubt, be more successful. The key word is commitment. You have to want it, stick to it, and be disciplined. In essence, *Decide Success.*

Exercise 4-a:

What can you be more successful at in your life by being better prepared? ☐

Chapter **5**
Raising Your Level of Intensity

"Always bear in mind that your own resolution to succeed is more important than any other."

—Abraham Lincoln

MAPPING PHASE
(1) Conduct an extensive assessment focusing upon interests, abilities, talents, strengths and weaknesses.
(2) Experience your own end-vision by actually projecting and engaging all your senses, and then identify the specific necessary steps to make it your reality.
WORK PHASE
(3) Put forth your absolute best effort—be resilient.
(4) Prepare and practice until you are ready, then prepare and practice some more—be diligent.
(5) Be so intense that you can feel a rush of adrenaline—be persistent.

The next of the Decide Success principles is a tough one to get. Let's start by throwing out words that start with "i." This is a very important success enhancer. You might put forth the following: Independence, initiative, and inspiration.

Perfection is the Only Option

Let me give you an example to help identify the next principle. When I was in my sophomore year of college, one of my friends mentioned that there was an EMT (emergency medical technician) class that we could take as a six-credit elective, so several of us signed up for it.

It was the first time I've ever taken a class where I didn't want just an A. I felt it was unacceptable to get anything but 100 percent. I had to get everything right. Why? Why did I have to get everything right in class? Because I would be dealing with people's lives! I couldn't go up to somebody who is in shock and say, "Oh, my gosh, I got that one wrong. Am I supposed to lift your head, elevate your head or feet, loosen your clothes, or put blankets on you? I don't know; I got that wrong in class."

It was not acceptable for me to earn anything but an A, anything less than 100 percent. Since then, I've had to help at accident scenes. I was in a Greyhound bus where we went off the road, and the driver was killed. I had to administer to him. People have fainted in my presence; it was good to know that I knew what to do until more qualified help arrived. So I felt a real need to get 100 percent in that EMT class. What word am I thinking about that starts with an i? *intensity*.

Football Championship Game Intensity

Here is another example of intensity. As I said, I coached seventh and eighth grade football. We went to the Toy Bowl, a city-wide championship game. My son was playing in the eighth grade. I was one of the coaches. I don't know a lot about football. I played soccer, as I said.

So, the first day of practice, the kids were goofing around, punching each other and kicking the ball. We had to bring them back together and constantly remind them that we were there to practice. Games were a month away. They were just being kids.

Contrast that to the day of the Toy Bowl. We went to Trinity High School stadium, where the game was to be played. We had a little pep rally first, then took a bus from where we practiced to the stadium. Not one word was spoken during the entire bus ride. These kids weren't goofing around, they were sitting quietly. We never told them to sit quietly. They were thinking about what they had to do that day. They filed off the bus without saying a word, no goofing around, nothing.

Intensity is focused passion and boundless energy. Tenacious, competitive, driven and persistent - that's intensity. As kids we used to call it "intestinal fortitude" (we were strange kids). Guts—doing that little something extra to win. The X factor. The will to win. Hunger. Accepting nothing less than victory. As the Oakland Raiders coined, "Just Win, Baby." Not only *Decide Success*, but make it happen.

My Parents: Forms of Intensity

Each of my parents is intense in their own way. My father needs to win. My mother needs to do her absolute best.

My father, the first John Baumann, had to win at everything he did. He was a high school baseball head coach for more than two decades. In fact, my mother would say one word to him as he left home on game day mornings: "Win." If you had the choice of a teammate in any sport, you were smart if you chose him.

For example, if you played golf with him as your partner and he was having a bad round, but your team had a chance of winning going into the last few holes, watch out. He invariably would do just enough to pull out the match; sometimes even shooting under par down the stretch. Some people fold under pressure, but he thrives on it. That is true intensity.

By contrast, my mother hates pressure, but she is intense in her own way. She would not describe herself as intense and she may not be in the traditional sense of the word. But she is just as intense as anyone. She graduated from Boston University in 1955. She commuted to and from school each day to her parents' home, which was more than an hour away south of Boston. The remarkable thing is that she was nineteen years old when she graduated from college!

Her will to do her very best motivated her (maybe also to get out on her own). She eventually became a college professor and, unlike many other professors, would improve her lesson plan each and every semester for more than sixty semesters. She did not get paid any extra for upgrading her plan. She just did it to do the best she could do. That is another form of intensity.

Competition and Intensity

"Intensity" or focused passion puts an emphasis on the competitive nature of school, activities, etc. I tried to figure out how I could get an A in each and every class. Learn the rules, stay within the rules, and use the rules to your advantage. I not only treated school like a job, but a competition. I treated the LSAT (Law School Admission Test) like a contest. I studied as hard as I possibly could to beat the other test takers and that intensity eventually paid off.

You may ask, "How is Intensity different from exerting effort or preparing and practicing? Let me use as an example my role as trial attorney for Exxon. Let's say that I was assigned a case that was going to trial and put out a tremendous effort as well as was as being as prepared as I could possibly be. My chances for success would be greatly improved, but something would still be missing. I would not have a job very long if I put out my best effort, was prepared, and yet lost every case.

You have to *want* to win. Really want to win. The missing element is intensity—caring about the outcome, having the intense desire to succeed. It is the emotional part of the equation. It's the fire. Determination! Effort and being prepared are the logical components of success. Intensity is the emotion.

Unlocking Intensity in Others

I had the great honor and pleasure of meeting the head football coach of the University of Louisville, Charlie Strong. He is an extremely impressive and enlightened individual. Charlie describes his role, not as an "Xs" and "Os" guy (creating and calling plays), as one might expect, but as a people person. He spends most of his time getting to know his players so that he can understand what actions he can take to get the most productive performance out of each player each and every game.

As he describes it, some players need to be called out in front of the whole team for their lackluster play to play better, while others would be totally demoralized by being screamed at in front of the team. Some players need to be privately challenged and others need to be constantly encouraged. The goal is for all players to peak in their intensity on game day.

Coach Strong said that his greatest challenge as a coach the year after Tim Tebow surprised many by announcing that he was returning for his senior year as quarterback of the national champion Florida Gators. Coach Strong was the defensive coordinator and all of his key defensive players were returning. The expectations were that the team would go undefeated and again be national champions.

The Florida Gators play in the Southeastern Conference, which has very strong football programs and traditions. Every week the Gators opponent is "up" for the game, hoping to ruin their dreams of an undefeated season. On the other hand, Coach Strong and the rest of the Florida coaching staff had the difficult task of motivating each and every player to play their best no matter who the opponent. Maintaining that degree of intensity was a daunting task. The Gators ended up losing in the Southeastern Conference championship game and were considered a one-loss failure as a team.

Motivations to be Intense

Awareness of what motivates human beings is an interesting area of review. What motivates? Truly motivates. Our entire economic system is based upon money as a motivator. Without money as an incentive, why would anyone dig ditches? Clean out septic tanks. Work in extreme temperature work environments, either hot or cold?

As with any motivator, there are positive uses of the motivation and negative uses. Selling books door-to-door, leveling the ground for above-ground pools with shovels, working through the night to complete a project with a deadline (each of which I have done) are all positive aspects of the desire for money. Robbing a bank is a negative aspect of ones desire for money.

Let's talk about motivation. What motivates people? What are the things that motivate people, what gets you to do these things, what motivates you? Wanting to be the best. Being the best. Excelling, okay, that's good. I've got a couple others in mind. Ever spend more time on something than it's absolutely worth just because you're what? Because you enjoy what you're doing? Having fun. What's the opposite of that? Anger.

Have you ever gotten on the phone with the phone company over a five-dollar overcharge, but, gosh, you spend an hour and a half with the phone company. What am I talking about? The principle? Anger, frustration, emotion. Emotions, they motivate. Now, punching someone out is a bad one.

Working hard to defeat them the next time or whatever, that's the good one.

You see it in sports all the time, offensive linemen or defensive linemen, when someone does something dirty to them, the next play, they do it clean, but they really take the guy out. Those are the rules. Anger is a good motivator.

Last But Not Least: Emotion as a Motivator

If you want to, you can take any situation and find a way to be motivated by it. I'll tell you the story about being the last person admitted to Cornell, which was an honor as well as an insult. That motivated me. That's a good thing. I was set to go to Boston College Law School when I received a call from the Cornell admissions office offering me the last spot. I asked how long I had to think about it, they said, the length of this phone call or they go on to the next name.

It was a Friday and classes started the next Monday. They also informed me that the law school dorm was full and I would have to find my own housing. I accepted, but asked if the dean of admissions had time to see me that next Monday morning. She did.

When I met with her, I first thanked her for admitting me. I also wanted her to know that she did me a huge favor by giving me the distinction of being the last one admitted. As Joe Namath guaranteed victory for the Jets in Super Bowl III, I guaranteed her that I would end up in the top quartile of my class. Talk about motivation.

Cherish Intensity

There are a few motives I want to mention. People are motivated by what they cherish, what is personal. It's okay to have those motives. It's not materialistic to pick something, and you don't have to be materialistic for the sake of being materialistic. I happen to love two things when it comes to materialistic stuff.

When I went to law school, you know, this is one of those stories like, yeah, I used to walk five miles to school in the snow with no shoes, uphill both ways. It sounds kind of corny, but I didn't have much money. I had to keep the heat down to save money, a few blankets on the bed; I didn't have a lot of material stuff.

As I said earlier, I thought about one thing that motivated me to be intense in law school. My future red convertible Corvette. Seven years after law school, I went out and found one that was two years old with 6,000 miles on it, garage-kept, and in perfect condition.

Here is the best part of the story. I went to see the car. The owner was asking below the Blue Book used car trade-in value, so something was fishy. I needed to know what it was. I didn't know if it was wrecked, flooded, what was going on.

We're sitting in this apartment in Brooklyn and I say to him, "You're not going to be able to sell this convertible until the spring. How much are you paying for storage—$150? Knock off $600 and we got a deal." His wife walks in from the kitchen and says very loudly, "That was a very good point." Then she walks out of the room.

I said, "Whoa, what was that?" He says, "We're living with her parents. It's getting a little bit tough and she wants me to get rid of the car, get the money to put a down payment on a house." I said, "Sold." I had gotten my answer. He was giving me a great price.

Where do you think that car is today? I bought it in 1993, it's a 1990 car. In my garage. I take it out about five days a year, it's in perfect condition, only has 50,000 miles on it. It's okay to cherish something if it motivates you in a good sense.

The only other material thing I have cherished, as I mentioned, was the five-acre lot I bought in Shelby County, Kentucky. I cut down fifty trees, which is dangerous and stupid.

You cut down a tree, and run when it starts to fall, because they fall whatever way they want to fall.

You can't control it. I live on that lot today, so that is something I cherish.

Legacy: A Motivator of Intensity

One more thing that motivates you to be intense is legacy. Feeling like you made a difference in this world. I know that sounds lofty, big, but that's one of the reasons I left the company I worked for over a decade. Why? Because I want to do this. I want to teach and I want to do inspirational talks. I want to write. I wasn't finding the time to do it. This is what I want to do, because I want to make a difference.

Another thing that I wanted to do was attempt to proactively eliminate harassment in the workplace—often it is sexual harassment. I found a way to eliminate it, if people will get me in there to do it. I call it my Proactive Prevention Culture programs. Where did this interest in sexual harassment come from?

When I was in college my roommate was this all-state nose guard, a big football player, not real tall, but big, a fire plug. He decided not to play football because he wanted to do other things. When we were juniors in college, he was on Phil Donahue talk show; he was a guest on the Donahue show because of some campus activism he was involved with.

He is now one of the biggest nationally known speakers on violence prevention. I say violence prevention, as opposed to preventing violence against women; because I've seen him speak so many times that it's a misnomer to call it violence against women. Men occasion 99 percent of the violence. When you say violence against women, it makes it a women's issue and it's really a men's issue.

It's not just the men who do it. It's the rest of us men who need to stop it, because we have mothers, sisters, daughters, that are being assaulted. We have to get in there and put peer pressure on. Be a vocal majority because, if anything, these violent men are giving the rest of us a bad name.

I've been motivated by that, I want to eliminate harassment. I want to use engaging imagery, real-life examples, and appropriate humor to persuade, encourage, and convince employees to prevent harassment in the workplace through peer pressure. My former roommate is out there trying to eliminate domestic violence, and other types of violence against women. Jackson Katz is his name. He's making a difference.

Top Gun Intensity

I love the movie *Top Gun*. In the class I teach, I describe the methodical approach of the "Iceman," compared to the more emotional, instinctive, fly-by-the-seat-of-your-pants approach of the "Maverick." In the movie, the character played by Val Kilmer, "Ice Man," flies jets by the book, making no mistakes, but showing little passion. Whereas, the character played by Tom Cruise has unbelievable talent and passion, but has some issues controlling his actions. You need both to really succeed at the highest level. Both are examples of intensity.

Raise your Hand: Intensity from the Get-go

Do me a favor: raise your hand as high as it can go. If you are in a car, open the window, and stretch your arm out the window as far as you can. Is that really the best you can do? *Now go a little farther.* You were able to do it, weren't you? Intensity is doing it all the way the *first* time.

Intensity in Sports

I'll give you another example of intensity. I'm going to use a couple of sports examples. I'm a Red Sox fan. 2004, Yankees, game six, who's pitching?

Why am I bringing up Curt Schilling? What's called the "Bloody sock game". Intensity. Just played right through the injury. Won the game the Red Sox had to win.

What else am I thinking about? Kirk Gibson. Why am I bringing up him?

Walk off home run. He had a leg injury. Came into pinch hit in the ninth inning of a World Series game, and hit a walk-off home run. He could hardly walk. Ends the game, wins the game. He has a hamstring injury—that's intensity. True focused passion.

Intensity: Asking Dirty Questions

I'll give you another example. I was reading a magazine that had an article about a guy who actually started his work life as a garbage collector. He asked a lot of questions and was really interested in the job and took it seriously. He even took the time outside of work to get his commercial driver's license.

His coworkers were thinking, "My goodness, you're a garbage collector. Pick up the garbage, throw it in the thing." Well, the driver didn't show up one day and who do you think they chose to be the driver? The guy who showed all the initiative. Exactly!

The same guy decides to learn about dispatching. He's asking all these questions about what they do, how they do it, like that. The dispatcher quits; who do you think they made dispatcher? Him! Goes on and on. He ends up being the CEO of the corporation. That's intensity. That's asking a lot of questions; that's taking it seriously. The guy in the article was a garbage collector, one intense garbage collector. One intense and extremely successful garbage collector!

The Hunting Dog: One Intense Animal

I'll give you one funny example. Maybe some of you have owned a beagle. Did he get out a lot? My beagle Max taught me more about intensity than any human being.

I would let him out in the backyard and he would get out. We had a fence and we would staple boards at the bottom of the fence and put up more fence. He got out every time from our backyard! He found a way. He knocked over the neighbor's garbage and I had to pick it up. I know that sounds goofy, but that's intensity. For some reason that hunting dog had to get out: he wasn't happy in that one spot. It was incredible how he would figure out a way. That's an example of intensity; a silly one, but an example nonetheless.

Famous Crime Fighters: Intensity with a Purpose

When you think of famous crime fighters, what do they all have in common? Intensity. Elliott Ness going after Al Capone. Melvin Purvis dogging John Dillinger. They had to achieve a result and exhibited focused passion.

Interestingly, both crime fighters had tragic lives after accomplishing their objective. Maybe they lost their purpose when they achieved their objectives. They lost their passion, their intensity, and their reason for being. They could find no pursuit that came close to what they have become famous for.

Top Athletes Starting Over from Scratch: Intensity

I am a friend of a University of Kentucky basketball star from a team in the 1970s, Jimmy Dan Conner. A number of years ago, he decided to revamp his golf game. His handicap was 7. Not 27, like mine, but 7. His average score was 79, or 7 over par.

You could see why he was upset. For the non-golfers out there, that was sarcasm. He didn't plan to join the professional golfers' tour. He just wanted to get the most from his ability. He started from scratch by working on a new swing.

During his first three months of lessons I understand that he didn't even touch a golf club. His handicap became a *plus* 2, meaning he averaged 70, or two below par, sixteen pars and two birdies or one bogey, fourteen pars and three birdies. When we play together, I get tired of saying after every shot, "Nice shot, Jimmy Dan." True intensity.

Another example is T. Will, Terrance Williams, a University of Louisville basketball star from 2006 to 2009 under Coach Rick Pitino. He was a high school star and the star of a top 10-college basketball program. He received lots of the ego-boosting attention; however, his coach pointed out that he actually lacked the ability to shoot. Did Terrence not believe the coach? Did he rebel? Did he just practice more? Nope. He worked to reconstruct his shooting technique. At first, he could not make a basket from a few feet away. Imagine how many times he was tempted to go back to his old, familiar technique. But he stuck with the new technique. He showed intensity. He was recently selected high in the first round of the NBA draft.

Blinker Story: Focus

People living in Louisville become very familiar with the horse-racing industry. If you ask a trainer why they race some horses with blinkers, they will tell you that some horses get distracted by the other horses, the crowd, whatever, and they lose their focus. The blinkers help keep them on track; excuse the pun. Maybe that is where the expression comes from. But they are better able to maintain their intensity. Focus.

Who are you? What Have you Done with my Father?

As I said, I learned intensity from my father. He was a competitive little boy in all respects. Still is. He loved competition, particularly baseball, so much that he became a high school baseball coach and continued as one from the time that I was a few years old until I left for college.

His competitiveness was so intense that after losing a close playoff game once, he was so preoccupied analyzing the game in his head that he took a wrong turn driving home. This was a trip he had made thousands of time before. On this particular trip, he drove the wrong way on the expressway for thirty miles and ended up in New York City before he realized his mistake. Now that is intensity.

Dad is in his seventies now. A funny thing happened recently when he invited me to partner with him in a Hilton Head golf tournament. I was excited to tell him that I was playing much better and my handicap had not caught up yet. He responded, "It does not matter if we win, so long as we have fun." All I learned from him suddenly flashed in front of my eyes and I naturally said, "Who are you and what have you done with my father?"

Do you agree that everybody can do the first five principles? *Decide Success*. Now, if this were one of my high school classes or groups, because I've done commencement speeches in high school for seniors, I would make you raise your right hand and repeat after me: I promise to assess, end-vision, put forth my best effort, be prepared and be intense in everything I choose to succeed at. But I'm not going to have you do that, because that's a little silly. But I thought you would enjoy that.

Life Balance: Intensity as a Choice

There has been much discourse recently concerning life balance. To me, keeping a good life balance is knowing when to be intense and, more importantly, knowing when not to be intense and just relax and enjoy.

Everyone has heard of, and knows, some type A personalities. These people are driven to be successful at everything they do. Being better than everyone else. Winning without regard for the impression that they are making on others. Going all out all the time. If that is what they truly desire, more power to them. Be happy. Most people decide to pick and choose what they truly want to succeed at doing.

Decide Success is designed to help you with those things at which you want to succeed. I have decided and my father has decided somewhere along the way, to pick and choose what we want to improve.

For example, I love golf. I love spending time with family and friends in a relaxed, scenic, outdoor setting. Winning, beating my best score, etc. is not a priority for me. I have other success priorities. You might say I have declined to *Decide Success*. I am not going to force myself to assess, go through the end-vision process, put out my best effort, work hard, prepare, practice, and raise my level of intensity with respect to golf. I just want to have fun and enjoy the activity, the day, the scenery, and the company.

In golf, great players actually remember and focus on the negative aspects of their round, while not-so-good players remember and focus on the positive. It's the opposite of what you might think.

When asked about a round, a scratch golfer will invariably point out the few bad shots. That's intensity and what they absolutely should be doing. Ask a not-so-good player, who is not looking to put in the work to succeed at golf, and they will re-live the wonderful drive they had on the third hole, the approach shot they stuck on the sixth hole, and that long snaking putt they holed on the 11th green. Interesting observation.Life balance is making the conscious choice what YOU want to succeed at and what you don't.

Adrenaline's Role in Intensity

This *Decide Success* principle is "Be so *intense* that you can feel a rush of adrenaline." Until now, I have not discussed adrenaline. I have felt the rush of adrenaline more in the last three years than ever before even with, and maybe because of, my Parkinson's.

My biggest symptom of PD is fatigue, described as the unpleasant sensation of lacking energy making routine activities, physical or mental, a strain. You may ask, "What does this have to do with adrenaline?" I have found that, while my body is releasing adrenaline, my fatigue is counteracted, or at least, postponed. I pay for it later, but I feel normal again, empowered, strong, full of energy.

What provides this rush of adrenaline for me? Inspirational presentations. As an attorney, representing underdogs who are being unjustly treated. Helping others. Feeling like I am doing something so unique to me that I believe no one could do it better.

Inspirational Presentations: Adrenaline

My first real talk was in Saskatchewan, Canada, for the rehabilitation workers, the Association for Rehabilitation Centers. The event was magical for me; it was magical for the attendees, they absolutely inspired me! I felt like I inspired them; people were hugging at the end of the talk.

During the hour and a half presentation, people were laughing hysterically; I was laughing too. We had people who cried at certain points as I talked about my daughter and her cerebral palsy and there was a standing ovation. We all wanted it to keep going as long as we could. It was over an hour of magical moments. These types of things don't come along very often.

Sometimes they come along in sports when someone wins the Super Bowl or the World's Series or something like that, or the World Cup, but it doesn't happen very often. If I can have that happen to me once every couple of weeks, once every month, or whatever, that would be something that would inspire me and feed this passion I have for inspiring people.

I love being on stage; I'm not shy about saying that. I don't script anything. I learned a long time ago not to read from a script. I need to flow with the energy of the moment and I love being on my toes. That's why I teach at the university and most of my teaching is critical thinking where I don't lecture, I debate with students. The most fun I have is when they're pounding me into submission as I take a position that is untenable, but that is fun because I get to think on my feet.

My first inspirational presentation of *You Ain't Dead Yet* was as the keynote speaker at the Houston Area Parkinson's Society Annual Education Summit. The talk combined my *Decide Success* principles with successfully living with a life-changing condition. I received a hand-written note afterward from the executive director saying, "You came, you thrilled, you brought people to tears, you brought people to laughter, but, most of all, you inspired."

I was on pure adrenaline during this sixty-minute talk before almost 500 attendees. Afterward, dozens of people came up to me with tears in their eyes, totally inspired to go on with life. I felt like a faith healer. I had used my God-given gift of relating to and inspiring people to the fullest.

My most memorable encounter was with an older gentleman who needed a walker and an attendant. He could hardly speak. He tried to say something to me that I could not understand. I asked his attendant what he said, and she had no idea. I leaned closer to try to hear what he was saying. Finally I could make it out. He was saying, "I ain't dead yet." Talk about warming my heart.

I hugged more people in pain that day than ever before in my life.

I paid for it later when the adrenaline wore off and all that fatigue caught up to me, but it was worth it. No doubt.

Find something to be successful at which causes you to release adrenaline.

Underdogs: Pure Adrenaline

As an attorney, I now represent what I call *legal underdogs*. I first need to be convinced that I am on the just side of a controversy. Then, I get involved if the economic resources between the parties are disproportionate. Finally, I look at the consequences of an unjust result on my underdog client.

My most recent trial involved me representing two forty-year old truck drivers, each of whom had a family with three children under ten years old. The transportation company that they had worked for accused them of stealing 125,000 gallons of fuel with a value of over $200,000. This was a civil, not a criminal action, so the standard for the jury was only "more likely than not." Was it more likely than not that these drivers stole this fuel?

The transportation company had three lawyers and a paralegal. My guys just had my wonderful part-time paralegal, Tracey Pender-Link, and me. We had them out-gunned for sure.

The most damning piece of evidence was a computer printout from the customer showing no short deliveries for any other driver over a seven-month period, except for sixty-four short deliveries by my two clients. And these supposed shortages were significant: typically half the load or over 2,000 gallons.

It was a jury-tried case. It was supposed to be a two-day trial and I committed to try this case on that basis. I knew my Parkinson's and fatigue would prevent me from any extended trial time. Unfortunately, the trial went into a third day.

On the third day, after the all the testimony had been presented, some procedural matters pushed our closing arguments to a fourth day. Unbelievably, in front of the attorneys, a representative from the trucking company, and my clients, but not the jury, the judge actually said that he expected a verdict in favor of the trucking company. You could hear the wind go out of the sails of my clients. In fact, they decided to drive three hours back to Nashville to be with their families that night.

I had no idea whether they would even show up for the closing argument the next morning. I went home and GOT INTENSE. I sat back and thought and thought. What came to me was that a trial is like a jumbled-up movie. One witness testifies about different parts of the story, all out of sequence. Then the next witness does the same and so on. A trial attorney's job is to unjumble the testimony into a story that makes sense.

I met my clients for breakfast the next morning; they had come back. I gave each a hug and said, "We won." Not, "I think we are going to win" or "I will do my best" or "Hope for the best," but simply, "We won." They asked if I had heard something from the court. I told them I had not. They asked to hear my closing argument and I said that they had to hear it fresh and live with everyone else.

I quoted the movies *Pretty Woman, My Cousin Vinny, Miracle on 34th Street,* and especially *Jerry Maguire*. Months later, I ran into the foreperson of the jury at a concert and he was nice enough to tell me that I rocked, whatever that means. My guys won, the verdict was unanimous.

The hugs exchanged were not the best part. The best part was when each of my clients walked off to call their respective families. You see, they were looking at financial ruin and personal bankruptcy if they lost. And this case had dragged on for six long years.

The strange thing is that I am convinced that, had we not had that extra night to prepare for our closing arguments, we would have lost. Intensity is sometimes equated with stamina. It was in this case.

Helping Others: Adrenaline

I also actually believe in my messages, I believe in helping people succeed, I believe in inspiring people especially in the healthcare profession. I believe in prevention, proactive prevention, preventing harassment in the workplace, preventing injuries in the workplace, and I believe in not having women be abused with domestic violence, in marital or other relationships. I believe in the mission of Make-A-Wish. So those are the things that I have determined are worthy of my time and effort and that's why I have focused on those. I have focused passion or intensity about all these things.

Be intense about something, anything. It is what makes life exciting.

Exercise 5-a:

Identify five situations from your life in which you have demonstrated intensity.

Exercise 5-b:

Identify the situations in your life where you have not been intense.

Intensity Creates Energy

Intensity generates energy and power to succeed. It is the fuel that allows you to exert your very best effort, and continue to prepare and practice when you are exhausted and want to stop. The true *Decide Success* formula has all these attributes: use your best effort, work hard, be as prepared as possible, and maximize your level of intensity.

I cannot emphasize enough that none of these steps require any special ability or talent—just commitment. Some would say discipline. Making the decision to do it! *Decide Success*. Just as in a successful diet or exercise regimen, the first few days are the hardest. Once you get into a routine or make it a habit, fewer and fewer actual decisions are made.

People who work at a traditional job get up every morning take a shower, get dressed, and go to work, usually without any specific decision-making. We just do it. Assessing, envisioning, exerting your best effort, being prepared, practicing, and being intense all simply take commitment to do so. *Decide Success*.

This should provide hope and optimism for those who want to succeed. Read no further. If you do all that has been described thus far, you will be more successful. I can guarantee it. Now, if you want to bring success to an even higher level, read on. The rest of the principles, though more difficult to adhere to and put into practice, can be accomplished.

PART 3

THE
ACTIVE
PHASE

Chapter 6
Seeking Out Experiences

"A man does what he must—in spite of personal consequences, in spite of obstacles and dangers, and pressures—and that is the basis of all human morality."

—Winston Churchill

MAPPING PHASE
(1) Conduct an extensive assessment focusing upon interests, abilities, talents, strengths and weaknesses.
(2) Experience your own end-vision by actually projecting and engaging all your senses, and then identify the specific necessary steps to make it your reality.
WORK PHASE
(3) Put forth your absolute best effort—be resilient.
(4) Prepare and practice until you are ready, then prepare and practice some more—be diligent.
(5) Be so intense that you can feel a rush of adrenaline—be persistent.
ACTIVE PHASE
(6) Continually seek out challenging experiences

Experience

You have to seek out as many experiences as you can. I would classify experiences into three categories: variety (related to what you decide to be successful at), stretch (not something you would normally do and that you feel some discomfort attempting), and life experiences (ones that you don't seek out, life just deals you, but from which you are able to gain knowledge).

Experience as an Attorney

One of the most critical areas in which you must gain experience is anything related to the career you have chosen. For me, it was as an attorney.

When I lived in New Orleans, I worked for Exxon and there were thirteen attorneys in the office. After two and a half years, learning as much as I could, I was finding that I only had work to do until noon each day. Sounds like a piece-of-cake job. I was earning a lot of money, working until noon, and reading journal articles in the afternoon. Instead of accepting the situation, I went to see the other attorneys, and asked, "Does anyone have work for me? I need to learn." They did not have any. What do you think I did?

I walked into my supervisor's office and I said I'd like to transfer somewhere else. I went a step further. I wanted to learn as much as I could, so I said, "I want to transfer to the most difficult assignment you can find." His response was, "Why don't you like it here?" I said, "I love it here." New Orleans. Who wouldn't love New Orleans? I said, "But there's not enough work to do; that's obvious, there are thirteen of us. There's not enough work to do for all of us; you know it and I know it. So I would like to transfer to learn, and get more experience as an attorney."

He called me in the next day, and said "Watch what you wish for: you're going to New Jersey, northern New Jersey, a refinery in Linden. You know, where the Sopranos are supposedly from. They show the tanks to a dirty refinery in the opening credits. You will be a labor lawyer and the teamsters are there, a thousand teamsters, and they have been there for fifty years. Plus, I'm going to let you do environmental work, Superfund, which is cleanup of hazardous waste sites. You will handle the Superfund cases."

All I could think of was, "Thank you sir, may I have another. " (An *Animal House* reference.) Why did I go from New Orleans to New Jersey? What did I ask for when I wanted to transfer? A challenge. Experience. Experience. I wanted as much as I could get. I was five years out of law school; I wasn't going to sit around all day.

What if my CEO came to me, said, "John, I want you to meet my nephew. He just graduated from law school. Could you work with him the next six months? After that, I'm going to pay you the same salary, but you're going to work in the mailroom. But teach him what you can teach him."

I'd leave that job in a heartbeat. Some people would say that's great, just do it. Sort mail for the same money. But I wouldn't gain any experience and you have to gain as much experience as possible. Think of what you provide to your employer: your time, your best effort, and value or work product. Now think about what you get in return. Not just money, but experience, and, yes, marketability. If either of the last two is missing, it's time to consider moving on.

Experience Develops Gut

Some years ago I was honored by the Kentucky Bar. They asked me to be a presenter to a mandatory course for lawyers who recently passed the bar. Talk about a tough audience. The new lawyers had to be there all day, for two days. No test at the end, just attendance. More than 250 in the auditorium. Egos all over the place. Know-it-alls. We went for the shock effect. My co-presenter's opening line was classic, "None of you have earned the right to say the words, 'my gut tells me...' you don't have a gut."

Guts take years to develop (ask many middle-aged men). Experience develops your ability to exercise judgment.

Experience at Formulating a Strategy

Every experience I have had in the field of law has provided me additional education. I worked in the district attorney's office one summer during law school. A tragic case went to trial that summer.

A man lost control of his car on the Long Island Expressway while he was driving home after having had a few drinks at happy hour in New York City. He struck a vehicle going in the opposite direction, and killed a baby and his young mother. The husband/father survived the crash. It was a clear case of vehicular homicide. However, the driver was acquitted at trial.

What happened? Is this yet another case where the legal system did not work? Actually, it was an invaluable lesson for me taught by the defense attorney. A less experienced criminal defense attorney may have brought the case to trial in the normal course of the process. The lesson was to always ask, "Who benefits from a delay?"

The case did not go to trial for more than four years. The driver made good use of the time between the accident and trial. He immediately started going to AA meetings, and was sober the entire time. When he was not working to support his stay-at-home wife and four children, he would speak to groups on the dangers of drinking and driving. The husband and father of the victims had remarried, and his new wife had a child on the way. The parents of the mother killed in the crash did not attend the trial.

However you feel about the result, you can appreciate the strategy of the attorney. This was a lesson that I learned because I was involved in the trial. Experience develops your ability to exercise better judgment.

Experience Gained from Observing Others

I had the privilege of assisting a prominent law professor, Charles Alan Wright, who Exxon had hired to argue an important case before the Fifth Circuit of the Federal Court of Appeals. The trial judge, after two days of trial, decided that the company suing my company had no case and found in favor of us for three separate and independent reasons. If we could get the Fifth Circuit to agree on one, we would win.

The judge included as many different reasons for his decision as he could think of. He was trying to make the possibility of success on appeal for the losing party so low that there would be no appeal. No appeal—no possibility of a reversal. (Lower court judges, especially federal court judges, hate to be reversed on appeal. They see that as an indicator of failure, and it is likely to be taken into account when the powers-that-be decide whom to elevate to the Federal Circuit Court of Appeals.)

In preparing the brief for the case, Professor Wright asked me to draft the argument in favor of the court affirming or agreeing with the lower court judge on the weakest reason of the three. I worked as hard as possible to come up with any plausible argument. On the day of the oral argument, approximately thirty of the top lawyers at my company were in attendance.

The panel of three justices consisted of two of the professor's former students at the University of Texas Law School. You could tell they had their knives sharpened, especially with respect to the admittedly weak argument I was assigned to write. In fact, Professor Wright did not get two words out before he was asked a pointed and very damaging question about the weakest basis for the judgment. His response was pure brilliance.

Instead of damaging his credibility in arguing for the court to uphold the judgment; on either of the other two reasons, he sacrificed the weak one by stating, "If it pleases the court, since the time I have for my argument is limited and the other two lower court reasons for finding in favor of my client are stronger, I would request that we not spend any of the court's valuable time on this issue."

You could see the air go out of the sails of the justices. No questions were asked during the remainder of the argument.

The opinion affirming (agreeing with) the lower court's decision addressed the weak reason by stating, "As virtually conceded by counsel at oral argument, the third basis for judgment does not apply; however, since the other two are valid, we affirm the lower court decision."

We won. The lesson: credibility is critical. Don't push an argument that is a clear loser unless you don't have a choice, and the objective is to win the war, not every battle. These types of experiences are invaluable in developing the ability to exercise good judgment, be adaptable, and be creative when solving problems.

Practical Experience: Sheriff at the Back Door

A particularly funny experience occurred my first week working as the attorney for a steel-processing company. I was visiting a plant when a sheriff arrived at the door with an attachment order. I thought it was too much of a coincidence and I was being set up, but it was legitimate. So I ventured into the fray.

A garnishment order had inadvertently not been responded to by the company and a court had ordered that a steel coil be attached (obtained) by the sheriff. I greeted him at the door and reviewed the paperwork. It was in order, but I asked him if we could deal with this when the court was open. He said he had a job to do. So I asked him which coil he wanted. He said any one would do.

I walked back to the plant manager, and informed the sheriff that we had to turn over a coil. He asked how the sheriff intended to transport the coil. So I went back to the sheriff and asked him. He pointed to a Chevy sedan in the parking lot. I walked back to the plant manager, and informed him that he had a car. He asked how the sheriff intended to secure the coil.

This was getting ridiculous. I went back to the sheriff and asked him. He showed me a rope he had. I walked back to the plant manager and informed him that the sheriff had a rope. He told me, with a coy smile on his face, to have the sheriff drive into loading bay #2 and meet him there. So I did.

When the crane operator started to lower a massive 40,000-pound steel coil onto the roof of the sheriff's 2,000-pound car the looks on our faces must have been hysterical and the whole plant came by to see the spectacle. The sheriff agreed to give me a day to call the court. This experience improved my knowledge base.

Exercise 6-a:

What additional experiences do you need to seek out to achieve the success that you truly desire?

Stretch Experiences

Many stretch experiences can be found within your success objective. "Stretch" meaning you are doing something outside your comfort zone.

When I was majoring in management at the University of Massachusetts, I had a unique outside work experience. I was promoted into a managerial position at a local restaurant when the other two assistant managers and the general manager walked out, while the owners were out of town, because of pay considerations.

I guess I was too green to be included in the plan. Presented with a situation like this, you do the best you can. I worked the entire weekend, and figured out what we needed to order from food suppliers. When the owners returned it was like the ending scene in *Home Alone* when the parents returned. It was a bit messy, but we stayed open and served the customers. I was definitely not in my comfort zone; in fact, I was scared, but I gained a valuable experience. This was another lesson in adaptability and self-confidence.

First Trial Experience

A major stretch experience was agreeing to be the lead attorney on my first trial when I was less than a year out of law school. A case was called to trial for an attorney who was about to go on a long-planned Hawaiian vacation with his family. It was on a Thursday afternoon when my supervisor offered me the opportunity. The trial was being held the next Wednesday, a mere six days away.

When I said yes, my stomach was in knots. It was a phenomenal experience, one that I have never forgotten. It is an experience that I have thought back to, drawn upon, and reflected upon many times when confronted with a new experience. I also gained additional self-confidence.

Experience as a Bookman

Selling books door-to-door in Houston, as I already described, was also a tremendous stretch experience. In fact, we had to find our own place to stay without spending too many of our hard-earned dollars. The book company gave us some ideas, one of which worked out.

My book-selling partner and I went to a local church and asked the pastor if there was a member of the church who had recently started living alone, and might appreciate company.

Enter Eda May Goode. Eda May's husband was in the hospital, and she appreciated our company. After all, we weren't exactly hanging around. As I said, we worked Monday to Saturday from 7:30 a.m. until 9:30 p.m. and had a sales meeting or fun event all day Sunday. She charged us each a whopping ten dollars a week. This stretch experience taught me resourcefulness.

Just like putting out your best effort, stretch experiences build self-confidence. For that reason alone, you need to venture out of your comfort zone.

An added benefit is that you may find a new passion. Have you heard the saying "I'll try anything once"? The one and only time that I will jump out of a perfectly good airplane included a lesson from a seasoned instructor. He told me that he had done his first skydive on a dare. Ten years later, he has had over 1,000 jumps, including two jumps where he had to use his emergency parachute. He not only found his passion, but learned from his experiences how important it is to properly pack both parachutes. What is a bucket list other than a compilation of stretch experiences? Some are planned for years, while others are done on the spur of the moment.

A Variety of Experiences

Without going into great detail, here are some of my stretch experiences that had no real connection with my success as an attorney: white water rafting through class five rapids in the Grand Canyon, skydiving just before my fiftieth birthday, driving a NASCAR on a track, swinging on a rope from tree to tree in Costa Rica, catching sailfish in Central America, deep-sea fishing overnight in the Gulf of Mexico, helicoptering over to an offshore oil rig, marshaling major golf tournaments (Ryder Cup, PGA, and Senior PGA Championships), playing on championship golf courses (Valhalla, Old Course at St. Andrews, Players Championship in Jacksonville), and riding a float at Mardi Gras.

Some unique experiences can be seen as stretch experiences because, even if you are not an active participant, you put yourself in a position to experience something unusual and special. Call them *Forest Gump-ish* experiences: seeing the Stones from the sixth row and also in a soccer stadium in Vienna, Austria; being in the pit during a NASCAR race; sitting at the scorers' table at a University of Louisville basketball game; going to a Super Bowl; going to a college bowl game; going to a Final Four; seeing Boston Red Sox games in as many ballparks as possible, including seeing Roger Clemens set the single game strike-out record; seeing a baseball division championship clinching game and a no-hitter; sitting in the front row of a concert (Pink Floyd and Kenny Chesney); being on the stage during a concert (Aerosmith); and going to the Kentucky Derby and sitting on Millionaire's Row.

Still on my list: go on a cruise to Alaska, live on the West Coast of the United States, and visit Amsterdam.

Never Stop Experiencing Life

What better way to seek out experiences than to actually live in as many different locations as possible. And when I say "different," I mean "different." First I lived in Long Island, New York, with its access to New York City: Broadway musicals, sporting events, concerts, tourist attractions, restaurants, and shopping yet, on the down side, little sense of community with each town melding into the next and a certain degree of constant tension, stress, even hostility.

Next I lived in western Massachusetts for college with its small-town feel and laid-back attitude. This was followed by Boston, Massachusetts, a city of neighborhoods and loyal friends, great historical significance, plus my favorite baseball team. Next, upstate New York on the Finger Lakes to attend an Ivy League law school with buildings truly covered in ivy. Not much to do but study, which was a good thing.

On to Houston, deep in the heart of Texas, a young, vibrant city with a great night-life, friendly people and good barbeque. Next stop, New Orleans, Louisiana; Mardi Gras, Cajun food, Bourbon Street, the French Quarter, a place like no other, a constant party. Contrast that with a move to Westfield, a bedroom community in northern New Jersey; very family-oriented. Finally my last stop, Louisville, home of the Kentucky Derby.

Although you can visit more places in your lifetime, nothing compares with the everyday experience of actually living somewhere. Living with people from different areas enhances your ability to successfully, "get into their shoes." This helps you to understand the actions of others and anticipate how they will react to a given situation—a tremendous advantage. A broad variety of experiences develops the ability to exercise good judgment.

Exercise 6-b:

What "stretch" experiences can you think of that would be outside your comfort zone?

Unintended Experiences

Some experiences are not sought out, but you can learn from all experiences. When I was diagnosed with Parkinson's Disease, I was told that the chemical imbalance in my brain due to the depletion of dopamine would result in depression. They were not kidding. I had never suffered from depression and had always had a pretty positive outlook on life. In fact, I could never understand why those who did suffer from depression couldn't just will themselves out of it.

Wow, was I wrong. I was driving the first time depression hit. Like a ton of bricks. I felt like I was in a deep, dark hole with no hope. No point in continuing to live. I just wanted to curl up into a ball and cry. It lasted twenty minutes, but it felt like twenty hours. When I came out of it, I felt the repercussions the entire day. I learned the true meaning of empathy.

The next time it hit was two weeks later. I felt the same, but I knew that it would subside. A horrific experience! But I might as well learn something from it. What did I learn? Compassion. Empathy. A better understanding and appreciation of what people with depression go through. How will that make me more successful? I have no idea. But everything happens for a reason. I may not know the reason yet, but I am confident that I will find out eventually.

Possession of Stolen Goods: Experience of Being the Accused

Another unintended, but valuable, experience allowed me to understand how intimidating it is to be interrogated by a person in authority. One Kentucky Derby, a law firm partner hosted me in a special seating area that included all food and drinks for the day. I arrived, presented my ticket, and was asked to wait off to the side for a moment. Two police officers almost immediately arrived and started asking me questions about my ticket.

When I told them how I got the ticket from a friend (a response I expect that they hear often), their interrogation became more intense. Turns out the ticket was stolen. Under the strain of the situation, I unintentionally made some minor inaccurate statements. I can now understand how people in custody could be thought to lie even when completely innocent. After all, I am a seasoned attorney, and I failed miserably. Talk about a learning experience. Again, I don't know what I learned this for, but someday I will know. I believe that every attorney should go through this experience.

Being Fired: A Surreal Experience

Some unpleasant experiences are also learning experiences that can help enhance empathy and perspective. I remember one incident that occurred about nine months after I started a new job. A senior executive tracked me down on a Sunday morning the day after a company event and, without explanation, directed that I come to his office at 2 p.m. that day.

I recreated all conversations that I had with everyone at the company function, and remembered that I had asked a salesperson whether he liked Alabama. I had heard more than a month before that he was to be transferred to Alabama. He expressed surprise and, although I tried to cover my mistake, he knew something was up. I was convinced that I was going to be terminated that Sunday afternoon for my loose lips.

I made sure I arrived early for the meeting and the executive's car was already in the parking lot; in fact, it was the only vehicle in the lot. I thought I was so fired. I did not have to experience it, I already had. I pictured it in my mind: the crushing nature of it, the undermining blow to self-image.

It turned out to be a personal matter, and he wanted my opinion, but I actually learned an invaluable lesson that day. I have had the responsibility to fire several people in my professional life. I know that I was more successful in doing the right thing with respect to how I accomplished the unpleasant task as a result of this experience.

I believe that honesty is underrated when it comes to terminating people. People want the truth. The truth allows people to retain some measure of dignity. Don't sugarcoat it. They need to able to be successful; they just no longer have the opportunity to do so at your organization. Don't think you are doing a good deed by telling them what you think will soften the blow.

As an employment attorney, I have always emphasized being honest. If you truly care about the people in your organization, you need to, I would even say have a duty to, provide accurate feedback. If an employee is not performing, give him or her a fighting chance by being forthright with him or her, not in a mean way, but get the message across in a clear way.

The words I recommend are, "You need to make an immediate and sustained improvement to an acceptable level of performance/conduct." This says it all. Immediate: Now. Sustained: Continuing. When it comes to "Acceptable," it is managements job to "Set and communicate expectations and consequences then hold all employees accountable in a fair and consistent manner."

One way I heard it put is, "We want all our employees to be successful, here or somewhere else." Some jobs are just not a good fit. Another way to say this is honesty is a gift rarely given.

Life-Changing Medical Condition Experience

Here is an article I once wrote about an unintended, life experience:

Muhammad Ali, Pope John Paul II, John Baumann, Michael J. Fox…Wait a minute; back up a name. What do I have in common with this group of famous people? You may have guessed it. The answer is that all these people have been diagnosed with Parkinson's Disease. Not many people outside the Parkinson's community know much about this condition. I prefer to call it a condition, but it actually is a disease, an incurable, progressive, neurological disease, which means that I am getting worse every single day I am alive.

Now that that horrible statement is out in the open, let me tell you what it actually is. A chemical called dopamine, which assists with coordination, is produced in the brain. When, for whatever reason, the brain slows or stops producing this chemical, and the amount of it left is reduced to less than about 40 percent of what is normal, symptoms start to appear.

For me, the first symptom was that my right arm did not swing when I walked. In fact, my friends made fun of my gait, not knowing that it was related to Parkinson's. By the way, it is very common for Parkinson's to be undiagnosed or even misdiagnosed by doctors, sometimes for years.

Over the next couple of years, other common symptoms of Parkinson's (referred to as PD in the community) appeared: less blinking, a poker face (small conciliation, but no one in my Texas Hold'em group could ever tell when I got that fourth queen); smaller handwriting and, finally, more and more, a shaking right hand.

I had injured my thumb playing goalie for the company soccer team, and thought that the shaking was nerve damage associated with the surgical repairs. When I went to the hand doctor, he referred me to a neurologist.

The funny thing about PD is that there is no test to determine if you have it other than doing an autopsy. Being that I am still alive and that I intend to stay that way for a long, long time, I opted against the autopsy.

Doctors have patients start the medication and see if the symptoms temporarily cease. If the medication works, you've got it. I hope you're learning something. Pre-PD, I had no idea about any of this.

Unfortunately, the medication worked. I am now a *Proud Person with Parkinson's*, which I think is a dumb label. Being from Louisville, I am a Louisvillian. Using the same logic, I intend to be known as a *Parkinsonian*. Thus, I am a *Louisvillian Parkinsonian*. Almost sounds like a scientist!

I have had many more experiences from wonderful to awful. The first key to being more successful is to analyze *all* your experiences to determine what you can learn and take from each and every experience.

The second key is to have many, many experiences. The consideration when deciding whether or not to go through an experience is what you will or may gain, versus what it will or may cost you. This is a cost-benefit analysis a risk-reward analysis.

Robbing a bank may have high potential gain, but the potential loss (potential loss of life, yours or others, and potential loss of liberty) always outweighs the gain. Whereas, taking on an assignment that is a stretch for you does have some potential risk (being fired); so long as it is fully communicated that the assignment is a stretch for you and that you are willing to take on the responsibility, the downside risk is minimized. Note though that the upside potential is unlimited.

Experiencing the Worst Thing

My son once asked me, "What was worst thing that ever happened to you." After thinking about it for some time, I said, "Nothing; she didn't die. Your sister didn't die." His sister was born with birth defects and given a 40 percent chance of survival. I imagined her funeral in detail, as excruciating as it was, maybe to prepare myself should I be forced to really experience it. It ended up being the best of both worlds; I got the perspective of what is truly important in life without the seemingly unimaginable pain of burying my baby.

Sometime later I asked a good friend the same question. He said, "My divorce." I reminded him that, if it were not for his divorce, he would not have met and married his current wife, and had his daughter, who is the light of his life. My follow-up question to him was, "Was the divorce the worst thing that ever happened to you, or the best thing?"

Often life experiences, however horrible at the time, often turn out to be valuable ones.

Exercise 6-c:

Think back to the most memorable experiences you have had and write them down here:

Exercise 6-d:

Have any of these experiences helped you to develop the ability to exercise good judgment?

Exercise 6-e:

Have any of these experiences helped you to develop your ability to adapt?

Exercise 6-f:

Have any of these experiences helped you to develop your ability to be creative in solving a future problem or issue?☐

Exercise 6-g:

Have you had any major life experiences from which you have learned a valuable life lesson?

Chapter 7

Developing Contacts and Resources

"In all our contacts it is probably the sense of being really needed and wanted which gives us the greatest satisfaction and creates the most lasting bond."

—Eleanor Roosevelt

MAPPING PHASE
(1) Conduct an extensive assessment focusing upon interests, abilities, talents, strengths and weaknesses.
(2) Experience your own end-vision by actually projecting and engaging all your senses, and then identify the specific necessary steps to make it your reality.
WORK PHASE
(3) Put forth your absolute best effort—be resilient.
(4) Prepare and practice until you are ready, then prepare and practice some more—be diligent.
(5) Be so intense that you can feel a rush of adrenaline—be persistent.
ACTIVE PHASE
(6) Continually seek out challenging experiences.
(7) Identify, develop and nurture extensive contacts and resources.

The seventh step has been discussed with renewed vigor recently, but has always been critically important in the pursuit of success: make and use contacts and resources. Whether through a business (LinkedIn) or social media (Facebook), or a rolling contacts file for your desk (for you youngsters, called a Rolodex), it involves collecting information related to the expertise of others so that you can call upon them, paid or unpaid, when needed in the future.

Contacts and resources, these are what are now called your "network." It's important to develop as many contacts as you possibly can and then find the resources, because that's often what you need in the business environment. You need to know who to go to and what they can bring to the table. And that value-added dimension sets you apart from other executives and other officers. Pay close attention to identifying and then actually nurturing your contacts and resources. In this day and age, nothing is more critical to success.

Step number seven, is about contacts, contacts, contacts. I'll say it this way: develop, maintain, and nurture a network of contacts and resources. Not as a means to an end, not to use or try to take advantage of people, but for mutual benefit or even altruistic purposes, get to know people. People like to do things for other people they like. So be a person that people like and don't ever lose your contacts.

I went to lunch once with Justice Scalia. I should have stayed in touch. He asked me to. I guess I was too busy. Doing what? Too busy to occasionally write a note to a Supreme Court justice?

As I said, I once worked a case with a famous law professor in Texas. We, or I should say he, argued before the fifth circuit in New Orleans and, until he died, we exchanged Christmas cards.

General Counsel: Job of Contacts and Resources

For over a decade, I was the sole in-house attorney for a publicly traded corporation. You will be surprised to learn that, although I typically put in fifty to sixty hours a week, I rarely did what you might think a lawyer does on a daily basis: perform research, write briefs or motions for court, draft memorandums, appear in court, etc. What I did was find the right resource for me to obtain the information I needed to provide necessary legal advice. That's it. I established a stable or network of outside attorneys who were specialists in the areas of law with which I might need help. This is a very valuable service I provide and it makes sense from an efficiency standpoint.

For example, for one securities law question, it would take me probably a week's worth of research to come up with an answer in which I may not even be confident. I could, instead, make one phone call to a securities attorney and, in five minutes, obtain the answer I need.

Contacts: The Impossible Reservation

What's the best restaurant in New Orleans? Ever hear of Commander's Palace? That's arguably the best restaurant. I had my going-away party there when I was moving out of New Orleans. The owners and I became friends during the years that I was living there.

When I interviewed with the CEO for the job in Louisville, we talked about New Orleans, and he said, "I'm going there for the first time in a few weeks." I sent him a note describing different places he might want to go. I didn't have the job yet, but it was probably a good move. I said in the note that it's who you know sometimes and that, if he needed anything, let me know, because I know a lot of people there.

Later I was paged. We had these stupid beepers back then: it would just come up with a number. You had to go find a phone and call the person. I called his secretary; she paged me and she said the CEO wants a table for eight. I said, "Okay, where?" She said, "Commander's Palace." I'm thinking, "I think I can do that." I asked, "What night?" She said, "Saturday night." That was a little tougher. What time? "7:30." Okay. Prime seating time. Anything going on that weekend? "Yeah, the SEC basketball tournament."

Wow. So I called up the maître'd'; he said no possible way. So I called Lolly Brennan White, a member of the family who owns the restaurant and said I needed a favor. I want to make a good impression, this is real important to me. I wanted to keep this job a long time. I said, "Can you do it?" She said, "I can't." I said, "Please, this is important to me." She finally said, "If I have to build a table myself and put it in the restaurant, you got it."

I sent her flowers the next day, and she knows she can call me any time if she ever needs anything. That's making a contact, maintaining it, and nurturing it. Keep track of the people you meet who are influential or will be influential. Get to know them. If you connect on a personal level, good, keep that connection. Handwritten notes are old-fashioned, but make people feel special.

Mystery Man

I recently met a man who was waiting to pick up a takeout order at a restaurant in Naples, Florida. He noticed that I had a reference to Louisville on my shirt and asked me if I lived there. I told him I did and we proceeded to have a very interesting conversation for close to forty minutes. We talked about Parkinson's, and about how having a positive attitude makes an incredible difference in overcoming adversity of any kind. I finally asked him about his connection with Kentucky. He matter-of-factly informed me that he was at one time the governor. He was the famous John Y. Brown, who made his fortune expanding KFC. He was also the former owner of the Boston Celtics, and was once married to Miss America, Phyllis George.

Governor Brown then asked me to contact a friend of his who was having a difficult time with his Parkinson's, which I later did. He also gave me his cell phone number to stay in touch, which I will. Contacts.

Realize that in every profession there are those that are great at what they do and others who are not-so-great. Great doctors, lawyers, electricians, carpenters, homebuilders, etc. Use your contacts to find out who is the best.

Favorite Day: Contacts can Surprise You

A company I represented was deciding whether to build a new plant in Alabama or some other location. The economics were tight, so the entire project depended upon how much we were offered in government incentives.

We had to appear before a panel of county commissioners. I checked around to find the most respected attorney in the area to be our local counsel, and determined that it was John Caddell. At the time, Caddell was in his early nineties. We show up for the hearing with our CEO in tow.

I consider myself somewhat of an expert in negotiations, so I started out by engaging in some small talk to warm up the panel and break the ice. It was college football season and being a fan, I threw out the tradition of the Alabama-Auburn rivalry. Bad move. The commissioners, to the person, expressed their loyalty to Alabama football, a couple of times even uttering the phrase, "Roll Tide. " Since they all liked the same team, I thought that I had dodged a bullet until *my* attorney, John Caddell, piped in, "Well, I am a huge Auburn supporter and, other than Auburn winning, my favorite day is when Alabama *loses*."

After semi-recovering from the kick to the shins that my CEO gave me, I asked for a short recess. When we got outside the hearing room, I frantically asked John what he was thinking. With a coy smile on his face, he informed me that he had known each of the commissioners since they were in grade school, even coaching some in Little League, and they all had the best interests of the community at heart. Nothing he said would affect that. We went back in and I felt a lot better about halfway through our presentation when one of the commissioners, while directing a question to John, mistakenly referred to him as coach. John Caddell was the right contact. The right resource.

Keeping in Touch with Contacts

With today's technology, there are no excuses for not developing or nurturing any contact that you identify. You don't have to occasionally meet them for lunch, although you should for important ones. You don't have to mail handwritten notes, although, as I said, this is a classy, extraordinary practice.
A simple single recipient email is sufficient. Picking up the phone is better, even if you leave a voice mail just to say hello and provide them the option to call back or not. A multiple addressee email, text message, Linked In message or comment from Facebook is not likely personal enough to qualify as maintaining a relationship with a contact.

Mentoring by Your Contacts

Why would someone in the later stages of their work life allow themselves to be a contact or resource for you? I mean, think about it, connections or contacts usually involve a tit-for-tat arrangement; you scratch my back and I'll scratch yours.

As Don Corleone said to the undertaker in *The Godfather*, "There may be a day, and this day may never come, when I ask you to return this favor."

You may not think that you have anything to offer. Be careful about not maintaining the relationship due to this perception on your part. I teach at the University of Louisville and usually have 120 students each semester. I am willing to help any student who makes the effort to get to know me. I have no ulterior motives. I just like to connect on an intellectual and friendship level with people in general.

For many people nearing the end of their career, the "giving something back" element outweighs the focus on constantly looking for the next promotion. For people in their fifties and sixties, it is often about positively impacting the lives of others. Successful people love to mentor or sponsor others. Be available for mentoring.

Look over the list of principles carefully. Do you see any steps that take any specific ability, talent, traits, characteristics, or intelligence? Not really. Anyone can do them. Do you see what I mean? *You* can be more successful. *Decide Success.* You don't need to be a rocket scientist to be successful. Just make the commitment to yourself. Decide. Follow the steps. Decide to be more successful.

Exercise 7-a:

Revisit step one (honest assessment) and identify contacts you have and resources at your disposal that could help you shore up your weaknesses. ☐	

Exercise 7-b:

Now identify contacts you have and resources at your disposal that could help you take more advantage of your strengths.	

Exercise 7-c:

Identify contacts you have and resources at your disposal in the areas of your interests (what you love to do).	

PART 4

THE EXPANSION PHASE

Chapter **8**
Increasing Your Level of Awareness

"An individual has not started living until he can rise above the narrow confines of his individualistic concerns to the broader concerns of all humanity."

—Martin Luther King, Jr.

MAPPING PHASE

(1) Conduct an extensive assessment focusing upon interests, abilities, talents, strengths and weaknesses.

(2) Experience your own end-vision by actually projecting and engaging all your senses, and then identify the specific necessary steps to make it your reality.

WORK PHASE

(3) Put forth your absolute best effort—be resilient.

(4) Prepare and practice until you are ready, then prepare and practice some more—be diligent.

(5) Be so intense that you can feel a rush of adrenaline
—be persistent.

ACTIVE PHASE

(6) Continually seek out challenging experiences.

(7) Identify, develop and nurture extensive contacts and resources.

EXPANSION PHASE

(8) Increase your level of awareness by (a) actively listening, (b) continually questioning what is,

(c)seeing beyond what is apparent, (d) proactively anticipating, and (e) learning from mistakes.

The eighth *Decide Success* principle is the most important one, by far. It doesn't come naturally for some people; you have to work at this one. This is something that some people never get and some people get easily, but everyone needs to focus on it. It starts with an a.

Anyone who has been out in public with a two-or-three year old will immediately understand the word hypervigilant. You try to know where they are every second. If they're out of sight for a split second, you panic.

Hide and Seek: Hypervigilance

I had such a situation. I was playing soccer, my son was two or three years old. My son was playing with a friend's two or three-year old son. His dad and I were playing soccer, messing around on Saturday afternoon. It was a little bit cold out and the boys had jackets on. All of a sudden we both look and they're gone. We were in a park. So, I looked at my friend, I said, "Where are Taylor and Joseph?" He said, "I don't know." We ran over to the side of the road and their jackets were sitting next to the road. The kids weren't around and we panicked. We started screaming and running around. It turned out that they were hiding under a bush watching us. It's amazing when you finally have young children at home or in a playpen, or somewhere that you can finally relax.

Awareness of Worth

There's a message in my favorite Christmas movie, "*It's a Wonderful Life*," with Jimmy Stewart and Donna Reed. George Bailey lacked awareness of what a difference he had made in so many lives, how many loving friends he had, and that he was truly "the richest man" in Bedford Falls. He had to go through the experience of seeing what life would be like had he never existed to realize what a wonderful life he had. Clarence, the angel trying to earn his wings, had removed George's blinders. How many movies and songs are about just that: seeing beyond what is apparent? Think about it.

Awareness in Country Music, of all Places

Next time you are listening to a country song, think about the message of awareness. Here are a couple of examples. In a song by Kenny Chesney, "There Goes My Life," a boy planned on traveling after high school, with his girlfriend. They end up having an unplanned baby.

The song starts out with him thinking that he ruined his life, but at the end of the song, he is seeing his daughter off to college and realizes that having her actually made his life worthwhile.

In the song by Sugarland, "Stay", a woman wants her married lover to stay and not go home to his wife, but the song ends with the realization that she is strong enough to end the relationship. These songs are about pulling off the blinders.

Awareness of Sixth Sense

Awareness. Have you ever waited tables? Think about what makes a good waiter or waitress. Having a good attitude and just being friendly, and having patience. Paying attention to what the customer's needs are.

Do you think the word "awareness" might come into play here? Think about how awareness plays in. The server watches to see if the customers have finished their drinks, and then refills them.

I waited tables in Boston for a year and I took it seriously. My ability to succeed directly translated into the amount of money I made in tips. I think I developed a sixth sense about customers and their needs. I was able to assess customers and their situations.

For example, these have been walking around Boston all day; it's a hot day, and they need water. These people are hungry and want their food because they're eating a lot of bread. This table wants to be left alone because they're being romantic. These people must have a play to go to, because they want out of here quickly. I learned to sense it. And I could, without looking, know where we were with each table. That's a sixth sense, if you take it seriously; that's awareness.

Awareness of Standing in the Shoes of Another

Why do I bring this up? It's like a game of chess. You have to plan ahead, look ahead, and put yourself in the other people's shoes; continually remind yourself to question why things are the way that they are. Become more aware of your world at all levels, from various perspectives, and put yourself in the shoes of others. That's awareness and it's very difficult to successfully do.

Increase your awareness by actively listening.

Awareness isn't something you can teach someone. It's something you need to focus on yourself and spend the time to understand. Talking, speaking, espousing what you already know helps others, but it doesn't help you grow and help you understand. There is much written about active listening. It basically is to let go of your know-it-all tendencies and respect the fact that someone else may have something to say that you have not thought of.

The simplest method that I have utilized to improve my active listening is to repeat back what the speaker just said to make sure I understood what they intended to relate to me.

Increase awareness by continually questioning what is.

When I talk about awareness, I talk about, "continually questioning what is." There are people who are naturally like this. So, if you want to succeed, ask as many questions as possible and, as they say, there are no stupid questions, there really aren't. If it's something you don't understand or know, even if it's on the most basic level, it's best to ask the question.

Ask lots of questions. Don't be deterred by the perception that you are a bother. You should always be asking questions and, if somebody is bothered by your questions, they're not the right person to ask. Spend time with people. Ask a lot of questions because you can only learn by asking questions and then listening to the answers.

Force yourself to continually question what is. Continually question what is. Don't take things for granted. Don't accept things just because an authority figure said it, question it. You don't have to be belligerent, you don't have to directly confront them, but you should, in your mind, question what is and say, "Did that make sense?" It will help you grow.

There are children who are naturally like this; they're always asking questions. I remember that scene from the John Candy movie, *Uncle Buck*, where John Candy asks McCauley Culkin what is his record for the number of questions he could ask in a certain time frame. That's a good thing for a child; it shouldn't be quelled, it shouldn't be quashed. It's a good thing for adults, as well, to continually question what is, to try to figure out why is it the way it is.

Increase awareness by seeing beyond what is apparent.

Once you've questioned what is and once you become more aware, the second part is to "see beyond what is apparent," see what other people aren't seeing, try to play chess, so to speak, look three moves ahead. Put yourself in the shoes of other people and see if you can expand your world and take your blinders off and see what is beyond apparent.

Try to put yourself in the shoes of every participant in a situation and see through their eyes. You'll see a different perspective and it will sometimes bring recognition of why something is happening or why something is confusing or doesn't make sense.

New Orleans Awareness

See beyond what is apparent. Remember my requested transfer from New Orleans to the most difficult assignment to obtain maximum experience? Well, there is more to it than that from an awareness perspective. Continually question what is. Why were there so many attorneys in that office? The answer is that there should not have been. It makes no economic sense unless the company was poised to acquire another company. But as the months went on, that explanation seemed less and less likely. See beyond what is apparent.

A successful company like Exxon is not going to do something stupid like having excess attorneys on the payroll for long. I started to consider job security. Which position has more job security? The one with the greatest workload, of course. Securing a transfer was one of the best decisions I ever made. Guess what happened a year later?

A year to the day that I transferred, Exxon closed the New Orleans law office and laid off all the attorneys, with few exceptions. They moved the work to Houston and these people had to find other jobs. That's awareness. That's basically saying, wow, something isn't right here. I better do something to control my life.

Seeing Beyond What is Apparent: J.A. City

The Louisville Junior Achievement has a new facility on Muhammad Ali and Fourteenth Street. The kids run their own city. One student is the mayor and one is the judge. For seventh and eighth graders, it's like a huge game of Life. You get a card. For example, you make $30,000, have two kids, have a budget, and have to make ends meet. It's really educational.

Texas Roadhouse built a facade and a little cafe area; the kids can even bake bread there. In fact, Thornton's built an actual gas station inside the building complete with pumps. Do you think JA paid Texas Roadhouse and Thornton's to put up the facades? The facade probably cost $200,000. What do you think JA kicked in?

It surprises many to learn that the answer is nothing. It's advertisement for the companies to be there. Really? So JA paid nothing? Do you think Texas Roadhouse paid any money? Yeah, in excess of $10,000 a year just to have it there. Thornton's did the same thing. Why would Texas Roadhouse pay that? Advertising! Why would they want to advertise to seventh and eighth graders? Because they will remember this experience when they're older.

Let me tell you something. I'm a parent of a nineteen year old and fourteen year old, I have not decided where we go to eat for the last seventeen years; the kids decide. We have gone to Texas Roadhouse about a dozen times since my son visited JA City. If he hadn't, we would probably not have thought of them. That's seeing beyond what is apparent.

Seeing Beyond What is Apparent: Books Target Parents

Remember I talked about the books I sold in Houston in 1980? Well, in essence, they were Webster's dictionaries with school study aids in the front. Maybe a four-page overview of algebra or biology. Much of sales work involves awareness, seeing beyond what is apparent.

The typical approach to selling these books was to focus on how they would help the student with the subject. And that goes just so far. But there is another audience for these books. Not so apparent. But once you bring it up, it may very well be the difference between closing the sale or not.

What audience am I referring to? I have one child who is a senior in high school and one in middle school. I believe that I should get a diploma for graduating elementary school three times. Once in 1971, again in 2004, and finally in 2009. Any parent who has helped their children with homework will understand what I mean. Who remembers this stuff? No, I am not smarter than a fifth grader.

I pointed out how the parents could use these books to refresh their memories and help out with homework. In sales, very often raising the customer's level of awareness is the key to making the sale.

Increase awareness by proactively anticipating.

I have talked about my unique harassment prevention approach. It is all about proactively anticipating. Here are the details.

In the workplace, the accepted approach for addressing discriminatory harassment, including sexual harassment, is to have someone in corporate human resources or a lawyer at a big law firm write a long, wordy, all-inclusive policy against such activity and then insert it on pages forty-five through forty-eight of a 100-page employee handbook. Most of the time, handed to, but not read by, new employees on their hectic first day of employment and then never referred to again until someone is accused of violating the policy.

Have these people ever questioned what is? Described this way, is there any wonder why harassment in the workplace continues? How does one "proactively anticipate" in this area?

I reproduce here an article I wrote for the American Management Association which focuses primarily on awareness and proactively anticipating.

In today's tough economic times, precious funds should not be wasted in defending cases claiming discriminatory harassment. These issues can be minimized or eliminated entirely—and critical funds saved for business operations with a program designed to build the right corporate culture.

The worth of such efforts may be seen in the example of one company with fifteen steel processing plants and 1,500 employees, of which 1,200 are on industrial plant floors. You would expect this type of organization to be involved with several harassment lawsuits per year. With a typical settlement likely to be in excess of $100,000 and the typical defense attorney fees to be an even higher amount, the unnecessary expense is substantial.

However, since 1999, this organization has experienced no employment-related lawsuits. Throw into the mix a diverse workforce (various religions, races, and national origins), and add women working on the plant floor, the record becomes even more impressive. Even more incredible is the fact that these plants are not limited to traditionally non-litigious locations, but this company's largest plants are in Detroit, Cleveland, northern Indiana, and Ohio.

How was this done and how can other organizations replicate these results? It was a matter of giving responsibility to the organization's first-line supervisors and hourly workers.

Proactive Workplace Harassment Prevention

1. Redraft your policy against discrimination and harassment to be concise and understandable. Using plain English, such a policy can be reduced to as few as 350 words and still completely cover all topics. After all, isn't this policy supposed to help the employees understand the organization's culture, and not be written so that only lawyers can understand it?

2. Communicate and fully explain the policy with descriptive examples to all supervisory and salaried personnel. Use real-life examples, or a variation thereof, to enhance the learning process. Use imagery to get attendees to feel what it is like to be the victim of harassment or discrimination.

3. Teach all supervisory personnel how to effectively communicate the policy to non-salaried personnel and require them to annually communicate the policy using a checklist. This demonstrates ownership in the program by a supervisor who is observed every day by hourly employees.

4. Teach all supervisory personnel how to effectively investigate a complaint. Company liability often results from an ineffective response to a complaint and an improper investigation of such complaint by organization personnel once they are put on notice.

5. Convince all salaried personnel that it is in their personal best interest to address a potential harassment situation even when no one is complaining.

Information, persuasion, reasoning, and involvement are the most effective means for obtaining ownership in any policy. Addressing issues early on is the best way to establish the right proactive prevention Culture.

6. Involve all employees in the program. A proactive prevention Program that involves all employees, both salaried and non-salaried, creates a culture that does not tolerate harassment of any kind and is the most effective program to actually prevent harassment in the workplace. Peer pressure and the negative reaction of co-workers to inappropriate language, the use of derogatory terms, and unacceptable jokes or slurs will do more than anything else to eliminate and prevent harassment in the workplace.

Proactively Anticipate: Avoid Regrets

All work-related fatalities should cause the owners and management of any organization to pause. Every one of us has an obligation and a moral duty to do what we can to prevent future fatalities by proactive anticipation.

I was at a charity golf outing one Monday afternoon when I got "the call." A truck driver had lost his load, resulting in the death of a mother of two young children. This call hit me as hard emotionally as any other issue I had to address in my professional career.

As I collected my thoughts, I remembered several times over the past year that I had thought of questioning the load securement assurance program. Perhaps I thought I might step on some toes, dislike the conflict, or believed that doing so was not *my* job. I regret to this day not actively engaging in the discussion. To prevent work-related deaths, raise your level of awareness by proactively anticipating, especially in the area of accidents. You may save lives.

Increase awareness by learning from mistakes.

An important, though often painful, way to gain experience that really hits home and often is a lesson never forgotten is to make a "mistake." Lessons can always be learned from mistakes and sometimes the long-term lesson learned turns out to be more valuable than the consequences of the mistake.

To use a sports analogy, if you never get up to the plate, you may never strike out or hit into a double play (failure, mistake), but you also will never get a hit or feel the exhilaration of hitting a home run (success).

Sugar Buzz: Inadvertent Mistakes

I remember an experience I had my first year as an attorney working in the Exxon office building in Houston, Texas. I had conversed often with the secretary of another Exxon attorney on my floor and had a somewhat relaxed relationship with her.

Our floor had a holiday party one December day with cakes galore. After the party, I was walking by the elevator when I noticed this secretary holding a bright orange envelope behind her back with the word "Confidential" written all over it in bold letters.

As she waited for the elevator among a few other people, I jokingly attempted to tug on the confidential envelope, pretending to try to take it. Unfortunately, I missed and my hand brushed her derriere. I was mortified. She turned and confronted me.

I learned a powerful lesson that day. No sugar at work. Not really. What I learned was work time is for work. From that day forward, I established an eighteen-inch rule while at work. Call it a personal zone so as to be sure to not make anyone uncomfortable. I also decided that I never again wanted to give another the power over my livelihood, and ability to provide for my family.

Successful Mistakes

In Louisville, Kentucky, Junior Achievement gives out the business Hall of Fame award. There is a committee that selects who gets this award. Every year they do a highlight video of the inductee's life, and then the person speaks. The recipient often doesn't know what to talk about.

One year someone suggested. "Why don't we do something a little different, not have them speak, not do the day-in-the-life video, but do an interview with them where they're comfortable. Don't ask them what their greatest accomplishment is, ask them what's the mistake you made that you learned the most from." The committee loved it.

The recipients also loved it because they're not patting themselves on the back; they're basically saying, "I am human." In fact, you want to ask this question of as many influential people as possible. That's the kind of information you need, because you want to learn from their mistakes, so you don't have to make those mistakes. To me that's critical, that's experience. Learn from your mistakes. You have made mistakes, I have made mistakes, and we are going to make more mistakes.

If you learn from them, that is what makes a difference.

Accidents: Learn from Mistakes to Avoid Future Injuries

In the safety realm, top executives talk a lot about safety. I only ask one question, "What are we going to do to prevent this from happening again?" You ask that for every accident.

Our injury rate went from 300 injuries for 900 people, in a steel processing center (we didn't make ice cream, although, I expect, that can be dangerous also), to sixty-two injuries for 1500 people. That's 400-plus people who didn't get hurt, but might have if we didn't do anything different, if we didn't learn from our mistakes. So learn from mistakes.

Seventh Circuit Case Mistakes: Trying to Do It All

Learning from mistakes is a humbling experience, because first you have to stop blaming others, stop making excuses and admit that you did your best, but made a mistake. If you need to, forgive yourself; it's nice to know you are still human. You are going to have to deal with the consequences, why not at least get some benefit from the experience? If you can do this, compliment yourself, you have a healthy ego, the right kind of self-esteem.

One mistake I made as an in-house attorney was thinking that I could do it all. Practice every area of law as well as the specialists in order the save the fees charged by law firm attorneys. We won a bench trial on an alleged national origin harassment case in northern Indiana federal court. I used local counsel who knew the judge, to avoid getting "hometowned." Too bad that I didn't learn the same lesson during the appeal.

The case was appealed to the Seventh Circuit Federal Court of Appeals in Chicago. It sounds impressive because it is. I had successfully argued an appeal in the Sixth Circuit in Cincinnati and assisted on ones at the First Circuit in Boston and Fifth Circuit in New Orleans. Minor leagues. This is Chicago.

Well, the attorney that lost offered to settle the case. We paid him $15,000 plus and had to forgive the $5,000 in court costs his client owed us. This was not a big-dollar case; in fact, the alleged victim had almost no damages. I got emotionally involved. As Mo Green said in the *Godfather* to Michael Corleone, "You buy me out, I'll buy you out." I pay him, he owes me.

I decided to argue the appeal myself to avoid additional attorney fees. Not to overwhelm you with movie quotes, as Julia Roberts said to the store owners who would not help her after her mega-shopping elsewhere, "Big mistake, Huge mistake. Huge." I got creamed.

The Seventh Circuit panel wanted to be addressed by known appellate counsel, not some real world in-house attorney trying to save his company a buck. The result was the Seventh Circuit sent the case back down to the trial judge for further fact finding. Now, me, being a typical hard-charging attorney, I never stopped to step back or consider whether I may have made a mistake not hiring some appellate specialist in Chicago who the Seventh Circuit would be comfortable with.

I did use my energy, intensity, focused passion (anger) to write the best, most complete post-remand brief to the trial judge. The judge provided more fact-finding and found in our favor again. They appealed. Did I learn my lesson? Did I even consider whether there was a lesson to learn?

Nope. I went ahead and addressed the same panel and we were destroyed. I learned my lesson. Use the people who do it every day. The Seventh Circuit ordered a new trial and the case settled at a reasonable number, but the lesson hammered into my head was invaluable. I am not now gun-shy, but there are situations where specialists are necessary and this was one of them. I painfully added to my experience.

A True Turkey of a Decision: Human Resources Mistakes

There is a well-known saying in the human resources world: "No good deed goes unpunished." Unfortunate, but often, very on point. I learned my lesson one November.

The year before, the company decided to provide a one-time special bonus of $100 to all employees because we had been more profitable than expected. The bonus was distributed with much fanfare as well as clear notice that it was a one-time special bonus and should not be expected in future years.

The following November, we received a number of employee inquiries as to whether a bonus would be distributed this year. Our numbers did not justify a bonus. The vice president of operations, who had decades more experience than I, suggested that we not respond to the employees and let it pass. I, being the human resources manager—having cornered the market on employee relations, insisted that we do something. I recommended that, with Thanksgiving coming up, we distribute $25 certificates that could be used to buy a turkey.

The vice president relented on one condition; that I distribute the certificates at the Detroit plant to the employees. Being a man of the people (remember, I had the title: human resources manager), I proudly accepted. I arrived at the plant that day and walked into a room full of stone faces. No one said a word as I distributed the certificates. Most of the employees did not show up to the "celebration."

Upon returning to the front office, I heard over the intercom someone broadcasting, "che-e-e-eap, cheap, cheap, cheap, cheap." Over the next four hours, I was serenaded with the same chorus over and over again. I guess the vice president was right. I certainly learned from the experience:

listen to those with more experience, put yourself in the shoes of others, sometimes it is best to say nothing at all, and no good deed goes unpunished.

Quite an eye-opening experience.

Exercise 8-a:

What mistakes have you made that you can learn from?☐

Exercise 8-b:

What mistakes have others made from which you can learn a valuable lesson?☐

Societal Awareness: Click it or Ticket

Once you start being more aware in career and business situations, you will not be able to stop. In society, there are many things that just don't make sense that you will start to see. See beyond what is apparent.

Think about the campaign to get drivers to wear seatbelts. The government is telling you that we are going to change your behavior, force you to wear your seatbelt when in an automobile, by fining you or taking some of your money, hard earned or otherwise. What does the government giving you a citation have to do with wearing your seatbelt, so that you are more likely to survive an accident? Does this make sense?

If the government wanted to see beyond what is apparent instead of doing what they have always done, why wouldn't they identify a more applicable consequence of not wearing your seatbelt? One of my favorite sayings is that the definition of insanity is to do the same thing over and over, and think that you are going to get a different result.

For example, why not do something that productively changes behavior like require that those who are not wearing a seatbelt to watch a film showing the aftereffects of car accidents at different speeds, the first half when seatbelts are not worn and the second half when they are worn. Clearly, following the experiencing of watching such a film, a violator's level of awareness will be greatly impacted; certainly more than writing a check to the government.

Awareness: Driving While Under the Influence

Seeing beyond what is apparent. Why would most people say that they are afraid of drinking too much alcohol and then driving? Getting a DUI if the police happen to pull you over. At one time you could get out of your first one. No more. You are talking thousands of dollars in legal fees, multiple classes, maybe suspension of your driver's license.

Now step back and think about it. Try to see beyond what is apparent. Is a DUI really what you should be concerned about? Really? What about ...oh, killing an innocent human being due to your impaired condition (this goes for driving on anything that impairs your senses). Forget the loss of liberty, horrors of jail time, financial burden, loss of employment, family disgrace, civil lawsuit judgment by the victim's family, etc., you took the life of another. Something you will have to live with the rest of your life.

To pile it on, you could also be responsible for the death of a friend, or even a family member riding in your vehicle. Let alone risking your own life. Makes you think.

Awareness: Societal Messages to Boys and Men

What message does society send to boys from the time they are able to walk or pick up a ball? Is intelligence rewarded? Is musical ability? Is artistic talent? What type of ability do you have to have to be popular or cool? The answer, as you know, is athletic ability. Why is this?

What is the next message that bombards boys as they become men? The better looking your girlfriend, the better you are; more accepted by the "in" crowd. Or how many woman you have been out with?

We are judged by what kind of neighborhood we live in, how big our house is, and what kind of expensive car we drive. Why is this?

Awareness means seeing beyond what is apparent. What I see is a flawed message being sent to boys. Once we become aware that the existing message is flawed, we can begin to send a different message, one that emphasizes the value of kindness, being a good friend, and giving back to society. This is an example of "shining a light on what is" for greater awareness. Often these are called, "*ah ha*" moments, those moments when you realize something that has been staring you in the face all along, but you have not seen it. There's no need to beat yourself up. Just decide to be more aware.

Personal Awareness: Truly Crazy

The same awareness you achieve related to your career, business, and society will become apparent in your personal life.

I'll tell you another story of awareness from Deepak Chopra. There is a researcher, twenty years old, in a subway. It's pretty crowded and this one woman sitting across from him that everyone was moving away from. She's got all the space in the world and it's really crowded.

He's questioning why this is. He hears her saying, "Well, I said, I said, I told her she should not do that; then she hit him, could you believe she hit him." She was talking to herself. He said to himself, "Where do people like this go?" When she got off at his stop, the researcher watched her; she went in the same building he was going into, a library. He lost her near the elevators.

The researcher then goes in the bathroom to wash up, and he's thinking, "I mean, what could she possibly be doing? Does she do this all day?" The guy next to him at the sink looks at him strangely and walks out—the researcher starts cracking up. Because he had been speaking out loud.

At that moment, the guy on the other side of him at the sink looks at him like he is crazy and walks out. The researcher had been laughing out loud at nothing. Awareness. He basically made the point that, he's a lot closer to this person than he thought he was. We all have voices in our heads; she just speaks them out. So did he. That's awareness. An "*ah-ha*" moment. Seeing beyond what is apparent.

Overboard Awareness: Lessons in Movies

Have you seen the movie *Overboard*? Did you like it? Goldie Hawn plays a champagne-sipping, snobby rich lady and she falls overboard one day and gets amnesia. Kurt Russell's character claims her and tells her that she's his wife, and they have three boys, and live in a shack.

She just goes on like she's the mom and gets engrossed in the life of mom and wife to this country bumpkin. Eventually she gets her memory back, and realizes she's rich, and not the boys' mother.

The reason I bring up the story is that Roddy McDowell, a very famous actor, took the role as her personal butler, Andrew. He had very few lines in the movie. I'm wondering, "Why did he take that role?"

There's a line in the movie that I think is the reason he took the role. It's such a profound line. After regaining her memory and returning back to the boat, Goldie Hawn's character is in the galley doing shots with the crew. She says to her butler, "Was I that bad?" And he said mimicking her, "Andrew, I've lost my diamond earrings somewhere between Fifty-first and Fifty-third streets, go find them."

She was devastated by how bad she was. She surprises him with the most heartfelt apology he has ever received from anyone. She said, "What am I going to do?" This is the line: he said, "Madame, we all go through life with blinders on. You have had the unique experience of having yours removed for a short period of time. What you do with that information is entirely up to you."

That's awareness. That's expanding your world, taking your blinders off. When I say take your blinders off, that's what I mean. Think about other people's perspectives, think about what else is out there, because we all have blinders. It takes real introspection and desire for anyone who has been in a certain social class their entire life to "see beyond what is apparent."

Awareness from a Dynamite Obituary

Sometimes awareness comes from the strangest places even when we are not looking for it. You probably are unaware that newspapers have already drafted obituaries for famous and semi-famous older individuals. Makes sense since we all will eventually die and there is no need to scramble for basic facts when they do.

Well, sometimes mistakes are made and obituaries are included in the paper prematurely. One such occasion resulted from the death of the brother of the inventor of dynamite. His obituary was mistakenly published, quite an eye-opening experience. It focused upon how many deaths and how much destruction had resulted from dynamite.

He took it as a "wake-up call," racking his brain for a way to avoid being solely remembered for dynamite. What did he do? He established an award to recognize humanitarians. The dynamite inventor is Alfred Nobel and the award is known as the "Nobel Peace Prize."

Awareness in Relationships

Finally, awareness comes in many other areas, especially in interpersonal relationships. Here is the "awareness" I have had concerning the committed partner relationship:

1. Don't expect a committed relationship to be successful until you are well on your way in

examining yourself and being comfortable with who you are.

2. Honestly and objectively evaluate your abilities and needs, and your partner's abilities and needs with respect to (a) ability to express appreciation, (b) ability to give and receive affection (c) ability to provide and receive affirmation of love for your partner (d) ability to be passionate and need for passion and (e) ability to share emotional, physical, and spiritual intimacy. Do your needs and abilities match?

3. In and out of the presence of your partner, affirmatively express and demonstrate a high degree of respect for your partner—never put your partner down. Do you think of your partners as a rock star?

4. Be your partner's greatest supporter and biggest fan.

5. Treat your partner with kindness at all times.

6. Give your partner permission to privately discuss with you ways you can improve yourself, and accept their comments as acts of love.

7. Settle for nothing less than everything—love is a soul's recognition of its counterpart in another.

8. Test your relationship by observing whether or not you and your partner cherish and love your time alone with each other. Be careful of the need to always find another couple to go out with.

9. Focus on developing similar interests so that you can do things together.

10. Commit to scheduling a set time each day to touch base and fulfill that commitment.

11. Have an agreement to check in with each other at least twice a week.

Awareness of the Importance of Professionals

A lighter example of awareness involves an encounter I had with a doctor once. As I mentioned, I played soccer. I once went up for a header at the same time that someone else did and we banged heads. Problem was his forehead collided with my nose. We all know who got the short end of that encounter.

So I'm at the emergency room with a broken nose. It is literally crooked. So the doctor examines me and gives me the option to be put under, with all that entails, or just having him adjust my nose in one quick, but very painful, move. I chose the quick route and, yes, he was right, it hurt like you would not believe.

So I get presented with a big bill for "surgery" and ask the doctor about it since it took him seconds. His response increased my level of awareness. He said, "Did you want just anyone, maybe one of your fraternity brothers, adjusting your nose, and take the chance of a permanently crooked nose, or someone with the experience I have?" I realized you pay for expertise.

Scranton Bus Accident: Awareness of Perspective

Awareness can have some detrimental effects as well. My first semester of law school, I received high enough grades to be offered a spot on Law Review; a high distinction and honor. I just had to receive the same grade point average the spring semester.

I went home between semesters and, when it was time to return to school, boarded a Greyhound bus in Huntington, Long Island, bound for Ithaca in upstate New York. It was a snowy, icy day.

Somewhere near Scranton, Pennsylvania, the bus went out of control and rammed straight into the trees that bordered the highway. The bus driver's head broke the windshield, and his legs were pinned by the steering wheel.

Being the only passenger with any medical training, I checked for a pulse; there was none. I then checked on the other passengers—nothing more than bumps and bruises. I then went back to the driver to make sure there was nothing else that could be done. I was not aware that dead bodies made noises, but they do.

Once I got back to school, I was still in quite a daze that lasted some time. I realized that there was more to life than law school. I had lost my edge. I was not as focused. I did fine my second semester, but not as well as my first semester. My increased level of awareness had affected my intensity.

Exercise 8-c:

List anything that you would consider an "awareness" or "ah-ha" moment you have had in the past few months.☐

Chapter 9
Trusting Your Instincts

"Follow your instincts. That's where true wisdom manifests itself."

—Oprah Winfrey

MAPPING PHASE
(1) Conduct an extensive assessment focusing upon interests, abilities, talents, strengths and weaknesses.
(2) Experience your own end-vision by actually projecting it and engaging all your senses, and then identify the specific necessary steps to make it your reality.
WORK PHASE
(3) Put forth your absolute best effort —be resilient.
(4) Prepare and practice until you are ready, then prepare and practice some more—be diligent.
(5) Be so intense that you can feel a rush of adrenaline
—be persistent.
ACTIVE PHASE
(6) Continually seek out challenging experiences.
(7) Identify, develop and nurture extensive contacts and resources.
EXPANSION PHASE
(8) Increase your level of awareness by (a) actively listening, (b) continually questioning what is, (c) seeing beyond what is apparent, (d) proactively

anticipating, and (e) learning from mistakes.
(9) Get in touch with, and trust, your instincts.

One example of trusting your instincts has been touched on earlier. It is found in the service you receive from an exceptional waiter. He seems to be aware of, and even anticipates your every need. Water is refilled when you are thirsty. He's there when you are ready to order. Brings the food at the right time related to the dinner conversation, and at the right temperature. Doesn't offer to clear the plates until you are ready. Presents the check when you want it, not a second before or after.

Once you are more aware, you can better anticipate what is going to happen, and then you can trust your instincts and make the most of what opportunities are presented in the professional environment.

Snowing in July: Instincts in a Crisis

I was working at a refinery on the New Jersey side of the Hudson River across from Staten Island, New York, and was called in one night at about midnight. The refinery had been shut down to make sure it was safe and to replace equipment that was wearing out. It was close to starting up when something called a "bed fluff" occurred. In essence, catalyst shot out of one of the stacks. Sounds serious.

My first question was, "Does the catalyst dissipate like smoke or something?" The answer was "no," it landed in Bayonne, New Jersey. I asked what part of Bayonne. The answer was, "All of it, we covered every house, car, lawn, and building with catalyst."

Wow. We had to address the situation and get ready for the media. What we found out was that, thank goodness, oil had not yet been introduced into the catalyst, so it was still just dirt or dust. It was non-toxic and non-hazardous clay.

We put ourselves in the shoes of others and tried to determine what their actions or reactions will be. What could we do for the residents of Bayonne before they woke up in the morning? Nothing about their homes, but what about their cars? The operations people somehow obtained the home phone numbers of owners of every car wash in Bayonne and bought out the car wash for the next week.

While we were considering how to get the message out, the media showed up. This was in July and they wanted to headline the piece, "Snowing in July." Fortunately, we had just finished media training. Our instincts told us to talk to the media. We were instructed to concisely answer every question, and then follow with our message, even if it felt a little goofy.

Why plug your message into every response? Think about it. How much of the interview makes it onto the news? The response to only one question. Not so goofy after all. Our message was, "I want to emphasis that this is non-toxic, non-hazardous dust and, for no charge, you can bring your car to any car wash in Bayonne this week." Because we anticipated that people might be concerned about their cars and provided a solution, no suits were filed. The only compensation was to those who were in the middle of painting their house.

The kicker to the story is that we estimated that 1,500 cars were affected. Know how many cars showed up? Over 4,000. People drove in from Jersey City, Staten Island, wherever, for a free car wash. Why not?

We tried to anticipate the impact of the dust on the residents, and anticipated that their biggest concern would be their cars. Our collective instincts were right on target.

In Charge of Exhibits: Instincts During Trial

I had the unique opportunity of trying a lawsuit with a famous trial attorney: Dick Miller. He is most famous for a case he lost. The verdict was in favor of Pennzoil against his client, Texaco, to the tune of $11 billion. Not million, but billion, dollars. It actually put Texaco into bankruptcy.

In our case, I was in charge of the exhibits. There were thousands of them. Dick Miller was brilliant, but just like many gifted people, was not always interested in the details and sometimes didn't pay attention when I was explaining something to him. Well, we named all the key exhibits. He started the first cross examination and, after about ten minutes, he walked over to me, put out his hand and asked for Mr. Evan's second affidavit.

Now, I had lived with this case for two years and I was listening to his questioning, and it seemed to me that he may have been more interested in Evan's fourth affidavit. But I was thinking that this brilliant trial attorney knew more than I did, so I handed him the second affidavit. He looked at it, then sternly back at me, and said quietly, but harshly, "I asked for his second affidavit." I immediately grabbed Evan's fourth affidavit and handed it to him. That was the one he wanted.

From that point forward, talk about pressure, I had to listen intently and anticipate where this attorney with thousands of trials under his belt was going with his cross-examination and go with my instincts. Give him what he wanted, *not* what he asked for.

I once read about a man who was listening so intensely to a lecture that he was actually sweating. This account was in one of my favorite books: *The Road Less Traveled* by M. Scott Peck. Well, sweat was literally pouring off my body at that trial. We got into such a groove that the other attorney stopped asking for documents; he would just reach out his hand and take what I my instincts told me to give him. I don't know to this day whether I was right every single time or whether he just went with what I gave him. Our instincts were in sync.

Unbelievably, the day after this cross-examination, the judge cut short this trial that was to last for weeks and reversed his prior ruling on a motion we had previously made to throw the case out. In other words, the case was over and we won. I had to enter the apex of trusting my instincts to meet the other attorney's needs. Like a blindfolded martial arts expert depicted in the movies, I got into the zone. A great experience.

Instincts of a Ship Captain

A friend who loves to crew on ships related a story to me of an exemplary captain with whom he once sailed. What made the captain exemplary? In one word, instincts. He would quiz my friend endlessly during voyages, asking him what would be on his mind if he were the captain. If a storm blew in right now, where would we go? What direction? What port? What actions would we need to take? If the ship's mast were to break or the engine were to fail, what is our contingency plan? He was in a constant state of utilizing his instincts. Lives were at stake, including his own.

Xterra Dents: Instincts in Negotiations

Here's another situation where instincts made a difference. I put an ad in the paper to sell my Nissan Xterra at a decent price, but certainly not a steal. This car truly was a beater. I got a call to look at it. My instincts told me what to do. The first thing I did was point out the dents to the prospective buyer; there was one at each corner of the car. I made him bend down and look at each one; some were more apparent than others. When he got in for a test drive, I told him that the car had no pick up and the gas mileage was awful. He looked at me like I was crazy.

Did I really want to sell this car? He asked me if there was anything good about the car. I pretended to consider for a moment and said, "The sound system is great." I then followed up with a question, "Why are you looking at Xterras?"

I did not tell him anything that he didn't already know or could see if he looked closely enough, but I built credibility by being upfront with him. He said that he liked how safe it was, because it was a small SUV on a solid truck chassis. Now the lack of pickup and gas mileage made sense. We made the deal. His was the only call I got on the ad in the paper and on the Internet for three weeks. Trusting my instincts was key to selling the car.

Instincts in Implementing a Policy Change

Another story of how instincts can be successfully applied to a situation is the implementation of a new, likely unpopular, company policy. My experience is that substantial time is spent on the decision-making process, yet little, if any, time is spent on the implementation strategy.

Here is a real-life example of how important brainstorming the implementation process can be. At a steel-processing plant with about a one-hundred employees, an anonymous letter was received naming two line workers and one supervisor as drug users. Our policy allowed for testing with reasonable suspicion. We decided that this letter qualified as reasonable suspicion and tested all three. One of the line workers tested positive and was dismissed. We went on to other issues.

About a month later, another unsigned letter arrived, this time naming thirty employees as drug users. We thought about testing all those who were named, providing education on the dangers of drug use, changing the policy, etc. After much discussion at the corporate headquarters, consensus was to institute random testing.

The decision-makers left the room without any discussion of how to best communicate this policy. One concern I had was that this plant had recently had a union try to organize it. I anticipated that company-imposed random testing would be a morale issue and could be used by a union as a rallying cry.

We put our heads together and decided that, rather than announcing this policy change by posting it on the bulletin board or having the general manager, who was not involved in the decision-making process, call shift meetings to announce it. Our instincts told us that we should discuss this policy change in a town meeting format.

We brought a copy of the existing policy and asked why we have a policy in the first place. As usual, no one said anything. For dramatic effect, we ripped up the policy in front of them and asked it another way, "Do we even need a policy?" Someone finally asked why the company feels the need to regulate recreational drug use outside of work.

We were prepared to address the "pot smoking on Friday after work with two days off until reporting to work on Monday morning" scenario. We had found a study where retired airline pilots were tested on a simulator and passed. They then smoked marijuana and took the test again. No surprise, they failed. They then waited two days and took the test again. Most of them failed again. The telling thing was that they had no idea that they were still impaired three days later.

After this story, someone in the back spoke up saying, "I don't do drugs. What we do is dangerous; we cut steel. I don't want the guy I'm working with to push a button at the wrong time and I lose my hand. I've seen it happen, and then find out later that he was on drugs. Why don't we have random testing?"

With some reluctance (not really), we suggested he start a petition. This happened at all three shift meetings. Over 70 percent of the line workers signed the petition. Random testing was instituted, the employees were a part of the process, and the union had no rallying point, all good. All because we had anticipated the reactions of employees and were aware of their feelings. We came to the decision for the right reasons: we care about the employees and don't want anyone to get hurt. Our instincts told us that, given the right information, our employees would come to the same conclusion.

Abusive Relationships: The Failure of Instincts

I was honored to be invited to do the opening inspirational presentation to a group of professionals and individuals involved in the domestic violence field. Lundy Bancroft facilitated a workshop based upon his book, *Why Does He Do That? Inside the Minds of Angry and Controlling Men.*

The theme was, "Time to quit wishing for a healthy partner who treats you well and stack the odds in your favor." The awareness I gained from the workshop was to beware of the person that you are immediately connected with or drawn to in a crowded room. Let your head into the selection process. In essence, learn when to not trust your instincts.

The other critical awareness for women was to pay attention to the reaction of a charming man when you don't want to do what he planned. If he is flexible, compromising, and accepts your decision, great. If he tries to shame, manipulate, and/or order you to go along with his plans, beware. Your instincts may not be in line with what is best for you.

Trusting Your Instincts

Once you have gathered enough experience, believe that you are prepared, and have increased your level of awareness, you have earned the right to trust your instincts. I am not talking about making "against the odds" decisions. I am talking about following proper instincts—doing what your gut tells you to do, now that you have put in the time and effort to develop the right kind of gut.

In Kentucky, there are two excellent basketball coaches, Rick Pitino and John Calipari. Each, without question, understands the game of basketball. Both make substitutions during a game with purpose—a real reason. A taller player when rebounding is needed. A three-guard set, if quickness and ball handling ability are required.

There are always occasions during a particular game when the coach just "gets a feeling" about a particular player and puts him in. Invariably, it turns out to be the right player at the time. No rational reason. They trust their instincts. Each coach has earned that right. They unconsciously anticipate which player is the right person to play at the time.

Parkinson's Attorney: The Role of Instincts in Direction

My instincts came into play when I realized that I should combine my extensive knowledge of, and experience in employment discrimination law with my intimate experience with Parkinson's. What a revelation.

While I would rather work with employers to help them do the right thing by complying with the law, I am poised to represent employees who are being discriminated against.

Exercise 9-a:

List successes you have had at using your instincts in the past few months. □

Exercise 9-b:

List times that you trusted your instincts in the past few months and indicate whether your instinct on each occasion served you well or not.☐

Exercise 9-c:

What can you do to increase your ability to improve your instincts?

THE LEGACY PHASE

Chapter **10**
Maintaining a Positive Attitude

"A pessimist sees the difficulty in every opportunity; an optimist sees the opportunity in every difficulty."

—Winston Churchill

MAPPING PHASE

(1) Conduct an extensive assessment focusing upon interests, abilities, talents, strengths and weaknesses.

(2) Experience your own end-vision by actually projecting it and engaging all your senses, and then identify the specific necessary steps to make it your reality.

WORK PHASE

(3) Put forth your absolute best effort —be resilient.

(4) Prepare and practice until you are ready, then prepare and practice some more—be diligent.

(5) Be so intense that you can feel a rush of adrenaline—be persistent.

ACTIVE PHASE

(6) Continually seek out challenging experiences

(7) Identify, develop and nurture extensive contacts and resources.

EXPANSION PHASE

(8) Increase your level of awareness by (a) actively listening, (b) continually questioning what is, (c) seeing beyond what is apparent, (d) proactively anticipating, and (e) learning from mistakes.

(9) Get in touch with, and trust, your instincts.
LEGACY PHASE
(10) Exude the most positive attitude possible.

What is a positive attitude? It is a life perspective that maintains a high enough level of awareness to seek out, search for, and dig deep to find a lesson, a positive side or outcome from any given event. It can simply be being more empathetic.

It is also a decision to *not* commiserate or wallow in your own or someone else's misery. There is a real difference between empathy or sympathy and enabling.

I used to debate with my former wife the whole negative / positive outlook thing. Her position was that she was just stating facts, which are neither positive nor negative, just facts. My position is that we can choose to identify, focus upon, and vocalize the negative facts or the positive ones in any given situation.

The glass that is half empty is also half full. That is why this phrase is popular. It points up the opposite ways to describe the same fact. Both are accurate.

As I mentioned, I was diagnosed at forty-two years old with Parkinson 's disease. It was a shocking and stunning development. I had always been an avid athlete; sports had always been a big part of my life. I played softball in Texas and I was actually the shortstop for one of the Texas State Championship softball teams. So, to some degree, I measured self-image, self-worth, and myself by my athletic ability, and then, all of the sudden that was taken away from me. Because, with Parkinson's, I can't throw a softball or baseball; I can't shoot a basketball; I can't serve a tennis ball.

There were other symptoms: hand shaking, an expressionless face, not blinking, and a softer voice. It was an interesting choice to become an inspirational speaker with these issues. It was a "welcome to your new reality" situation. I can't say that it didn't throw me for a loop, because it did; it would throw anyone for a loop.

It's what I've done with that since then, and that is developing my inspirational speaking business. I speak on Parkinson's; I speak about my daughter who has cerebral palsy and how it is to be a care receiver as well as a caregiver, and, in fact, caring for the caregiver and caring for the care receiver. I speak on how to be successful at Living with a Life-Changing Condition. Entitled, no surprise here, You Ain't Dead Yet.

A positive attitude can result in being successful or not, just by the way you view things. As I discuss in my "Reclaiming Posi-spective" inspirational presentations, having a positive attitude has been proven to have a beneficial effect on illnesses, including mine.

What is the placebo effect in clinical trials but believing that the pill you are taking will help you in a positive way? This is a well-documented and accepted fact. In essence, those who received no medicine in the study still had measurable beneficial improvement.

Maintain a positive attitude or "posi-spective." That is, keeping a positive perspective, and setting your goals high. Someone once said to me, "If you don't have any expectations, you can't be disappointed." That's a pessimistic way to look at things. It may be true, but then you won't be striving for stretch goals. I like to say that if you reach for the stars and don't quite make it, you're still in the heavens.

Becoming a Proud Person with Parkinson's: The Role of Attitude

Remember my story of unintended life experiences when I was diagnosed with Parkinson's, a progressive, degenerative, incurable disease? Needless to say, a positive attitude can be tested at times.

Once the shock started to wear off, I got proactive. I learned as much as I could about PD. I was asked to be on the board of the Parkinson Support Center of Kentuckiana. I went to the World Parkinson's Congress in Washington DC.

Talk about supportive, my seventy something year-old parents drove from their home on Hilton Head Island and sat through a bunch of hyper-technical lectures just to support me. That's love.

What I learned was that there are some brilliant people working on a cure. More than five years ago, they said that a cure would be discovered within five years. I guess some scientists have trouble with basic math, but, come on team, get going with it. My quality of life depends upon it.

Next, I learned there is something that I can do. Although the progression of the disease can't be stopped, it is possible to slow it. Wow! That was what I was hoping to hear; talk about motivation. Every Parkinsonian progresses at his or her own rate. Since I am not a medical researcher and it's too late to go back to school, I am not going to find a cure. However, I may be able to affect my quality of life.

This list may not surprise you: exercise, eat right, take supplements, reduce stress, be optimistic, laugh a lot, stretch, and get lots of affection (not really, but it can't hurt). I need to be in tune with my body and involve my movement disorder specialist to regulate my medications. By the way, eating right includes blueberries, strawberries, and (no kidding) red wine and dark chocolate. Say no more; I am signed up.

My next decision was to do something that I felt would be more worthwhile with my life than being a general counsel for a publicly traded corporation. Despite much apprehension, I recently started up my own inspirational speaking firm, The Inspiring Esquire. See more at:

www.JohnDecideSuccess.com

In addition, I opened a legal/management consultant and speaker business, Proactive Prevention Culture, I dedicate my energy and passion to eliminating workplace harassment, providing supervisor leadership skill training (including avoiding unionization), reducing workplace injuries, and teaching success and negotiation skills. I speak, when asked, on Parkinson's.

Ted Williams: Mr. Attitude

I may be biased, being a lifetime Boston Red Sox baseball fan, but I believe that Ted Williams was the best hitter ever. He may not have had the lifetime statistics that some other hitters had, but Ted Williams fought in two wars and missed many of the prime seasons of his career.

Whatever you think of Ted William's arrogance, and he certainly was that, he is a perfect example of having an attitude that motivated him to be the best he could be. He is quoted as saying, "All I want out of life is that when I walk down the street, folks will say there goes the greatest hitter that ever lived. I think he was. So does my brother Ted. And he is not even a Red Sox fan.

Katie's Election Speech: Maintaining a Positive Attitude

Here is a speech written by my thirteen-year-old daughter. Katie was born without a diaphragm and her lungs had no room to develop while she was still in her mother's womb. She had to be delivered six weeks prematurely and put on a life-support machine that circulated her blood in and out of her body to remove carbon dioxide and replace it with oxygen.

Whether due to this process or as an independent medical condition, she has cerebral palsy. In her school, seventh and eighth graders can run for office. As a seventh grader, she delivered the following speech:

> In case you do not know me, my name is Kathleen Mary Baumann. I am in the seventh grade and I am running for safety patrol leader of Student Council.
>
> I would like to be your safety patrol leader because I want to show people that I am more than just the girl with cerebral palsy.
>
> I have a voice and I want to use it for the middle school students of Summit Academy.
>
> I also want help the community especially by having a canned food drive for the homeless and abused women and children.
>
> The reason I would be the best SPL is because I have been able to overcome many obstacles in my life.
>
> I want to fight for the flag just as much as I had to fight to live and that is why I have the strength to be safety patrol leader.
>
> Okay, now I want to know how many people like sweets here? Well then, wouldn't you want to have a bake sale to raise money?
>
> How many people like recess and loft? I am prepared to suggest that any money made from the bake sale be used to buy new loft and recess equipment.
>
> Another service project is raising money for the shelter dogs by selling Friday free dress day passes for a dollar.
>
> I hope you will trust in me that I will work my hardest, just as much as I did to live, to do whatever I can to make this school the best it can be.

Is there any doubt who won the election? What more can I say about how essential a positive attitude is to success?

Miracle on Ice: Collective Attitude

In the 1980 Olympics, the Russian team, made up of professional hockey players, were overwhelming favorites to win the gold medal. During the warm-up exhibitions, they destroyed every team they played including the American team, which was made up of all amateurs, mostly college players. Herb Brooks was the coach of the U.S. team.

The Americans barely made it into the medal round, and were set to play the Russians in the first game of two games. The U.S. team was down in the final period of the game, but had hung with the Russians. You could sense that the longer they stayed competitive, the more confident they became, and the more negative the Russian players became.

When the US team took the lead in the final period and won the game, the victory became known as "The Miracle on Ice." Was it a fluke or an example of the effect of having a positive attitude? Herb Brooks will tell you that it was all about believing that they could do it. Nothing is impossible. Maintain a positive attitude. Every player on the team was convinced that they could, as a team, beat the Russians and win that game.

Attitude in the Face of a Life-changing Medical Condition

How Can You Stay Positive When You Have Parkinson's Disease?

By Richard London

The emotions I experienced when I was first diagnosed with Parkinson's Disease were a mixture of shock, fear, and relief. The relief came from finally knowing the cause of the symptoms I had been experiencing for years and in getting medication that actually helped control them. It has been five years since that diagnosis and I have learned a lot about Parkinson's Disease (PD) in that time, more than I ever wanted to know.

Chances are that you already know that PD is a degenerative neurological disease with a variety of symptoms that can be quite frustrating, and sometimes debilitating. Everyone is affected by PD differently, but I believe that there is one thing in common that all of the people I have met with PD have who are still getting out and enjoying their lives.

They *choose* to have a good attitude and make the most of every day. When I say that they choose to make the most of every day I mean exactly that. I know people with PD who seem to always smile and are a joy to be around. They seek out new activities so they can continue to feel productive in their lives.

We can all be overwhelmed by life's challenges at times. I know there have been times that I have felt like I deserved a good pity party. When you feel that way I have some advice that might surprise you. My suggestion is to have your pity party. Have a real good one. Spend ten minutes complaining to yourself about all of the problems in your life. Make a list of all of the things that frustrate you, but limit yourself to exactly ten minutes.

Then start a list of all of the positive things you have in your life. Write down the names of the people around you who love and support you. Write down all the activities you enjoy that you can still do. Take stock of your blessings and remember that there is always someone out there who has it worse than you do.

Then look back at the list of things that frustrate you and ask yourself how important each item is in the big scheme of life. For those issues that really bother you, ask yourself, "What can I do about this?" Remember the Serenity Prayer, "God grant me the serenity to accept the things I cannot change. The courage to change the things I can, and the wisdom to know the difference." Accept the things you cannot change. There's no sense frustrating yourself by trying to change them. Acknowledge that some things in life are outside of your control and focus on what you *can* do.

One of the things that has worked wonders for me is staying physically active. I can't do everything that I used to do, but I push myself to do what I can. Find an activity that you enjoy and push yourself to do well in it. My wife and I started taking ballroom dancing lessons. She loves it and I do the best I can. Tai Chi is a wonderful activity to develop balance, coordination and mental focus. Whatever you decide to do, do it on a regular basis to keep your body and mind active.

Another choice that you have is to volunteer to help others rather than focusing on yourself. Remember what I said, there's always someone out there who has it worse than you do. By focusing on someone else I found that besides my having the satisfaction that I am helping another person, I am more conscious of the blessings in my life.

In summary, choose to live every day to the fullest. Stay active to keep your body and mind sharp. Take your eyes off of yourself by helping others. In short find a way to enjoy life to the fullest every day. I think you'll agree that it's better than the alternative.

Richard London is a person with Parkinson's, seven-year cancer survivor, and has had nine surgeries following a life-changing automobile accident. He is a public speaker and author of *A Handbook for Life: A Practical Guide to Success and Happiness* (www.AHandbookForLife.com). He has a commercial pilot's license and a third degree black belt.

Katie the Cheerleader: Unmatched Attitude

Another example of how a positive attitude is essential and can be inspiring to others is my daughter's decision to become a cheerleader in the sixth grade. She had been reluctant to get involved in the fifth grade, because she was concerned that her cerebral palsy would prevent her from doing the cheers. She was also concerned that other children would make fun of her if she fell or could not do the cheers properly.

I was surprised when she announced that she was going out for the cheerleading team. As a parent, I never want my children to be hurt, whether physically or emotionally. I was very concerned until I saw how excited she was to be a cheerleader. The smile on her face made up for any missteps.

The next year, she announced that she no longer wanted to be a cheerleader. My reaction was a mixture of relief and disappointment: relief that she would no longer be exposed to possible injury or teasing; disappointment that she may have given in to the naysayers. To my amazement, she finished her announcement that she was trying out for the girls' basketball team instead. The power of a positive attitude is inspirational.

Attitude of a Wish Child

A positive attitude can actually extend one's life. For quite some time now, I have been involved in the Make-A-Wish Foundation. It did not dawn on me until very recently that there are amazing similarities between my "Reclaiming Posispective" presentations for care receivers, family care partners, and professional care partners, and the mission of Make-A-Wish.

In my talks, I let care partners know how much they are appreciated and how their positive attitude does more to maintain a care receiver's quality of life than any medicine. With Make-A-Wish, I have seen first-hand how "the wish" actually adds time to a child's shortened life. Here is a note from the regional office that illustrates one of many such examples:

Hello everyone,

I have some extraordinary news! Our wish child that I wrote to all of you about yesterday will have her wish granted tomorrow! Through all of your efforts and the compassionate network of emails you all must have sent out, I was introduced to a company in Cincinnati. They manage fleets of jets for many corporations and private owners. They sent out a message to their owners and one of them had a flight going to LA tomorrow morning. They are stopping in Cincinnati to pick up our wish child and her family in a G550. Her doctors have helped us arrange all of the oxygen concentrators for the flights and she is ready to go.

The outpouring of support has been overwhelming. I have had calls and emails all day from people who wanted to help. Her wish to visit the beach and some of the sights of Los Angeles has inspired so many to give, suggest leads, and send out the message to others.

Thank you all for caring so much. She has been told how many people have cared to make a difference in her life and she is touched beyond words. You have all jumped through hoops with your care for one child who matters and now she knows she matters.

For all of you who pledged funds for her wish, thank you so much. Obviously we do not need the funds now but your generosity was so moving and I appreciated your outpouring of support!   Thank you,   thank you,   thank you...you are all AMAZING.

(Before the wish week, this wish child was given three weeks to live. She lived four.)

Exercise 10-a:

Is it more natural for you to be an optimist or pessimist? Explain.☐

Exercise 10-b:

Describe some situations in the last few months where you adopted a negative attitude, and the outcome might, just might, have been better had you maintained a positive attitude.

Chapter **11**
Uncompromising Integrity

"It takes twenty years to build a reputation and five minutes to ruin it. If you think about that you'll do things differently."

—Warren Buffett

MAPPING PHASE
(1) Conduct an extensive assessment focusing upon interests, abilities, talents, strengths and weaknesses.
(2) Experience your own end-vision by actually projecting it and engaging all your senses, and then identify the specific necessary steps to make it your reality.
WORK PHASE
(3) Put forth your absolute best effort —be resilient.
(4) Prepare and practice until you are ready, then prepare and practice some more—be diligent.
(5) Be so intense that you can feel a rush of adrenaline
—be persistent.
ACTIVE PHASE
(6) Continually seek out challenging experiences.
(7) Identify, develop and nurture extensive contacts and resources.
EXPANSION PHASE

(8) Increase your level of awareness by (a) actively listening, (b) continually questioning what is, (c) seeing beyond what is apparent, (d) proactively anticipating, and (e) learning from mistakes.
(9) Get in touch with, and trust, your instincts.
LEGACY PHASE
(10) Exude the most positive attitude possible.
(11) Live up to a standard of uncompromising integrity.

One of my heroes, who is also a Parkinson's champion is Muhammad Ali. He writes in his book, *The Soul of the Butterfly,* "At night when I go to bed, I ask myself, "If I don't wake up tomorrow, would I be proud of how I lived today?"

You need to hold yourself to a higher standard. Don't ever compromise when it comes to integrity, and that's a personal choice. Of course, you have to comply with the law, but often you need to go well beyond the law, and the law doesn't always catch up with ethics and morals.

Front of the New York Times: Integrity

What is integrity? Living up to your word. Meeting your commitments by being where you say you will be when you say that you will be there. How many of us meet these standards? Think about it. Do we do this? Go over in your mind your actions of the last forty-eight hours.

One simple approach you can take is to ask yourself if what you are about to do ended up on the front page of the *New York Times*, would you be proud or ashamed? If you would be ashamed to see it on the front page of the paper, don't do it. On the other hand, if it's something you'd be proud to see on the front page of the paper, go ahead and do it. If proud, do it. If ashamed, don't. Simple.

Momma Test for Integrity

The same test can be applied to disclosing what you are about to do to your mother. If she were to find out, would she be proud of you, or embarrassed and humiliated. It is that simple.

White Lies: Can they Exist in a Life of Integrity?

White lies—is there anything wrong with white lies? Do we tell them to protect others because we are so caring or to avoid confrontation? Better to make up a story than to have to reveal the true reasons. How kind. Can you appreciate my sarcasm? A lie is a lie is a lie. Once you rationalize that a lying is sometimes acceptable, even the "kind" or the right thing to do, you have blurred a line that can never be brought into focus again. M. Scott Peck wrote in *The Road Less Traveled*, "The fact that a lie is white does not make it any less of a lie or any more excusable. "

If It Feels Right: Integrity

A formula for success can also be described as follows: find out all the rules, abide by the rules, and use the rules to your advantage, if it feels right. This is where integrity comes in.

Clean up on Aisle Everywhere: Integrity in Business

Here is an example from the environmental law realm. Before environmental laws were passed, people would dump awful stuff into lakes, rivers, onto the ground, and there was no regulation against it. That doesn't feel right; they shouldn't have done it, but it wasn't against the rules or the law.

Many people have heard of Love Canal—an entire community built on a toxic waste dump. The people involved in burying the barrels of waste had to have known, on some level, that they were doing something wrong. It could not have felt right in the pits of their stomachs. They did not violate any laws when they did it, but the legal system often lags behind morality and ethics.

Good People at Their Worst: Failures of Integrity

I once heard a divorce attorney say that she has found that people going through divorce are "good people at their worst." How people behave during a divorce is a true indicator of integrity.

I have been in the process of divorce over the past three years. Due to the instability of my medical condition and my ex-wife starting a career, we have had to continue our financial relationship as a sort of joint venture. There have been testy times, but for the most part, we have maintained a good working relationship.

My perspective has always been: why do married individuals have to go directly from love to hate. Isn't there a way to back down from love to being close friends? Now, I know all the reasons why that rarely happens: hurt feelings, dashed expectations, maybe you were never friends in the first place, etc. But if it is any example to others in this situation, my ex-wife and I are close friends, not for the sake of our wonderful children, but because we shared almost twenty years of our lives together. We have shared special moments and have great memories.

What I discovered during the divorce process is that there are many opportunities to hide cash that would certainly never be detected. The person taking this road could rationalize putting aside some money by convincing himself or herself that the system is flawed anyway.

A person with uncompromising integrity would not do so. Not because they may get caught, but because it does not feel right. Don't believe rationalizations. Don't buy into the excuse that everyone does it. Although hiding some cash did occur to me, I made the decision throughout to take the "high road." In doing so, I can look myself in the mirror without being ashamed. It is not a fear of being caught. It is a decision to do the right thing.

Integrity is often thought of from a religious perspective in a "thou-shalt-not" way. Heaven vs. hell. A humorous quote from Mark Twain comes to mind. When he was asked about where he would rather go, he responded, "I don't know whether I would rather go to heaven due to the climate or hell due to the company."

I prefer to look at integrity from a positive, "thou shall" perspective, rather than a negative, "thou-shall-not" perspective. The Golden Rule. Do unto others as you would have them do unto you. Take affirmative action as opposed to refraining from doing a list of "don'ts." My former wife and I used to debate the difference between being kind as opposed to not being mean. She believed that there was no difference. My position is that there is the world of difference. One requires affirmative action while the other simply refrains from doing something. To be truly successful, integrity must encompass both sides of the coin, refraining from taking certain actions, as well as affirmatively taking actions of integrity. Examples of integrity include giving back to the profession, community, society, etc.

Insider Trading: More than Just Integrity

I recently analyzed an insider trading case. It provided more practical and economic reasons for not engaging in insider trading. Some officers of a company were told that the company was going to be sold for 50 percent more than its current public trading price. They allegedly bought a number of shares before the announcement.

Let's conduct a cost-benefit or risk-reward analysis. On the benefit or reward side, they each realized a profit that equaled the cost of a small car. Now let's look at the complete cost or risk side. First, they were risking years of sleepless nights hoping that they never get caught. Second, they risk public humiliation if they do get caught. Third, both of the above may affect their marital and family relations. Fourth, they risk a civil complaint being filed by the Securities and Exchange Commission to recover the ill-begotten gains, which presumably they have already spent, and would need to take out a loan to cover. Fifth, fees paid to a defense attorney. Sixth, any costs, penalties or fines assessed.

But there is more: Seventh, the possibility of a criminal indictment, including jail time. Eighth, being fired. Ninth, the inability to find a comparable position, especially one that involves trust.

I bet none of these individuals considered what compromising their integrity really involved. The lesson here is that even someone who has no integrity, and is willing to engage in insider trading may be dissuaded after completing a risk-reward analysis.

Live up to Your Word: Integrity

I referred to my New Warrior training earlier. At that training, I also realized much to my embarrassment and chagrin, that I was not living up to my word. My word, whether in the form of a commitment, promise, oath, or statement, meant very little to me.

A life of integrity draws no distinction between any of these words. If you say that you are going to do something by a certain time, you either did or didn't live up to your word. No excuses allowed. Were you on time or not (whether late or even early)? I was playing fast and loose with my words. I would over-commit and call to say I would be late. Sometimes just not show up. This is not living a life of integrity. To be truly successful, you need to mean what you say and say what you mean. Your word is everything.

Exercise 11-a:

Over the next week, make note of each occasion where you did not live up to a commitment you made.□□	
Date	Occasion/Circumstance

Exercise 11-b:

Over the next week, make note of each occasion where you told anything other than the absolute truth.☐

Chapter **12**
Having Faith

"Faith is taking the first step even though you can't see the whole staircase."

—Martin Luther King, Jr.

MAPPING PHASE
(1) Conduct an extensive assessment focusing upon interests, abilities, talents, strengths and weaknesses.
(2) Experience your own end-vision by actually projecting it and engaging all your senses, and then identify the specific necessary steps to make it your reality.
WORK PHASE
(3) Put forth your absolute best effort —be resilient.
(4) Prepare and practice until you are ready, then prepare and practice some more—be diligent.
(5) Be so intense that you can feel a rush of adrenaline—be persistent.
ACTIVE PHASE
(6) Continually seek out challenging experiences.
(7) Identify, develop and nurture extensive contacts and resources.
EXPANSION PHASE
(8) Increase your level of awareness by (a) actively listening, (b) continually questioning what is, (c) seeing beyond what is apparent, (d) proactively

anticipating, and (e) learning from mistakes.
(9) Get in touch with, and trust, your instincts.
LEGACY PHASE
(10) Exude the most positive attitude possible.
(11) Live up to a standard of uncompromising
integrity.
(12) Have faith in yourself, in others; in a higher
power and believe that your life has purpose.

Last one. What could it be? As George Michael would say, "You gotta' have *faith*." I cannot believe that I quoted a George Michael song. Faith and having faith that there is a reason for everything that happens! Having faith that God wouldn't give me something that I couldn't handle; having faith that there is a higher power that will guide me through these barriers and detours.

Do a revised assessment and new end-vision. The point is that doing an honest self-assessment and then creating an end-vision for yourself is not a one-time thing. It is something that needs to be done on a regular and continual basis.

Have faith. In yourself. In others. In teammates, your work team. Your family. And, last, but certainly not least, in a higher power.

Confidence of Others: Faith

I was approached by my litigation section supervisor about whether I felt ready to try a lawsuit when I was about nine months out of law school. The problem was that he approached me on a Thursday and the trial was scheduled for the next Wednesday.

It was a busy six days. I ended up writing a fourteen page opening argument that Clarence Darrow, a famous trial attorney, would have been proud of. When I stood before the judge, paper in hand, and started to read it, he stopped me almost immediately. He said in a booming voice from high up on the bench, "Counselor, what have you got in your hands?"

I said, "My opening argument, your honor."

"How many pages is it? "

"Fourteen."

"You going to read it? "

"Every word, " I said proudly. It was that good. He then asked if I knew the case. I told him I did.

He ordered me to put down the paper and just tell him in my own words what the case was about. I explained that the person bringing the lawsuit claimed that we did something to cause rainwater to flood his neighboring property. I told him we would be able to show that the four corners of the client's property are higher than his and rain has always flowed that way. He said, "Thank you, now sit down."

The valuable lesson I learned from this experience was to keep it simple and never read to a court, jury, or audience. What sustained me throughout the process was the faith that my supervisor had in me even if I did not yet have it in myself.

Sugarland: Faith in the Goodness of Others

I went to the state fair in Kentucky with my fourteen-year-old daughter. After changing careers, I found myself in some financial difficulties. I determined that, although we wanted to see the concert by the country music group Sugarland, I could not justify spending $100 for a pair of tickets.

My daughter and I stood outside the facility and simply asked, as people went by, whether anyone had any extra tickets. We did this for about thirty minutes with no success. My daughter started to lose patience and faith. She was ready to give up. I encouraged her to remain positive and not lose faith. After all, we did not need hundreds, dozens, or even multiple concertgoers to help us out, just one. When I turned back to ask the next couple passing us, they stopped and looked at each other, then turned to us. It just so happened they had won four tickets in a radio station contest and only needed two. My daughter's face beamed as they handed us the tickets. Excellent seats. We both had a faith experience.

Innocent Sons: Faith that Justice would Prevail

Another story of faith is about a woman who had to experience the pain of having two of her sons go to prison for murder. She lived her entire life in the small central Michigan town of Gaylord. Despite two separate juries finding her sons guilty "beyond a reasonable doubt," she never lost faith. As a character says in one of my favorite movies, *Miracle on 34th Street*, "Faith is believing when common sense tells you not to." She never lost faith. Not even for one second.

Ester's son, Laurie Moore, was arrested in what the authorities called, "a drug deal gone wrong." Rather than resolving an unsolved murder, it was only the start of a seventeen-year saga. The case involved misconduct by government officials, and witnesses who were pressured to perjure themselves.

County Prosecutor Norman Hayes filed murder charges and Laurie Moore was convicted of involuntary manslaughter with a sentence of seven to fifteen years in prison. Hayes also filed charges against Terry Moore who was convicted of murder, as well. Murderous brothers, rivaling Jesse and Frank James, had been brought to justice. Or had they?

In the years that followed, facts emerged that implicated Hayes had exhibited severe and reprehensible prosecutorial misconduct and had had a personal vendetta against Laurie Moore. Hayes not only had issues with Laurie Moore from high school, but Laurie had, years earlier, married Hayes' former girlfriend.

Eventually, evidence that had never been produced for defense attorneys, was inexplicitly discovered by the state police. Further, the eyewitness charged that the government had coached her and confessed that she had lied. After spending three years and eight years behind bars, respectively, Laurie and Terry Moore were released from prison and the charges were dismissed.

Ester never lost faith. That is what having faith is all about.

Ending a Long-term Relationship: Faith

I believe that one must strive to be as selfless as possible in almost all areas of life. However, I believe that in one area it is absolutely acceptable to be selfish: the decision to spend, or not spend, the rest of your life with someone in a life-partner relationship. For the partner who does not provide monetary support of the family, the leap of faith is even greater. You are likely looking at a significant reduction in your lifestyle. Faith is the belief that "things will work out" despite there being no guarantee that everything will be taken care of. Faith is following the first eleven *Decide Success* steps and knowing that there is a higher power looking out for you.

Another in Need: Faith that a Reason Exists

Faith is also seeing things in a more expansive way. I could not locate my wallet the other day, so I grabbed a hundred dollar bill that I always keep in my house in case of an emergency (or my absentmindedness). I put it in my pocket and did not need to use it all day. At the end of the day, I reached inside my pocket for the bill and much to my chagrin it was gone. I checked my car and it was nowhere to be found.

..........I believe than anyone, no matter how much money they have, would be upset about losing such a bill (maybe not Bill Gates, but us normal folk). What surprised me was my reaction. I actually smiled and thought, "Well, someone needed the money more I did."

..........Where did this faith come from? My grandfather came to mind. As I mentioned earlier, he owned the corner store. From time to time, for family functions or the like, he would leave the store in the hands of someone else. These were the days of cash transactions and no credit cards or computers. Sometimes those people entrusted with the store would rob him blind. On several occasions, I heard my grandfather say, "Well, they must have needed the money more than I did." Faith.

Against All Odds: Faith in Others

It was a day that we had waited for. The day that we would learn the gender of our unborn baby. The ultrasound had been scheduled for almost a month. We had a five-year-old boy and, although I really had no gender preference, since my wife had trouble with both of her pregnancies, it was possible that this would be our only other child, so a girl would be nice.

The nurse ushered us into the examination room and started the ultrasound machine. There was a distinct hum from the machine as the nurse spread gel out over my wife's six-month pregnant midsection. I was smiling from ear to ear as we happily conversed with the nurse. Images came up on the monitor and the nurse explained what each image showed. Finally, the nurse had a view that allowed her to determine the sex of the child: a girl. I felt so full of love that I teared up.

Since an ultrasound has other medical purposes, the nurse continued to talk to us as she ran the device over my wife's belly. Suddenly, the nurse stopped talking and a grimace came to her face. She said, "I need to get the doctor" and left the room. We were blown away. From the highest of highs to the lowest of lows.

After a few minutes, the nurse returned with the doctor and they had a conversation as if we were not even there. The nurse said, "Do you see it?" The doctor at first replied, "No, " but then said, "Oh, now I see it." As the shock wore off, I finally asked, "What is going on?"

The doctor explained that our baby had a hole in her diaphragm. My first thought was, "Is that all? Can't you fix it?" He went on to explain that there is no pre-birth procedure to repair the diaphragm and the hole was allowing her stomach to move up into the space where her lungs need to develop. He recommended a specialist, Dr. Sheldon Bond.

We met with Dr. Bond and the first thing he told us was that our baby had a less than 40 percent chance of survival and, even if she beat the odds, there likely would be other medical issues. He explained that we had alternatives to going forward. I did not want to hear it.

I come from a family of fighters and had absolute faith that my child was a fighter. We would do everything possible to help this baby survive. Faith is a powerful thing. It motivates. It propels one to do their absolute best. It provides life force energy. It allows one, by sheer willpower, to overcome all odds. Success for me was the survival of my daughter, and I was not going to let anything stand in the way of that objective.

I also had faith in my doctor. My initial somber meeting with him described was tempered by my reaction to his name. It was wildly inappropriate given the circumstances, but I was laughing hysterically inside. A scene from the movie, *When Harry met Sally,* became stuck in my mind. Harry, played by Billy Crystal, asked Sally, played by Meg Ryan, if she ever had had great sex. Sally said rather emphatically, "Yes." Harry would not let it go and asked, "What was his name?" Sally replied, "Well, if you must know, Sheldon." Harry burst out laughing and said, "A Sheldon can do your income taxes. If you need a root canal, Sheldon's your man. But humping and pumping are not Sheldon's strong suits. It's the name. Do it to me, Sheldon. You're an animal, Sheldon. Ride me, big Sheldon. It doesn't work."

Well, that is all I could think of. Something about Sheldon Bond told me not to look any further. That, in fact, he was "my man."

The one thing about Sheldon Bond is that he lives in a world where babies that he is trying to save die. I realized that how he deals with that is by not making eye contact with the parents. What scared me most was that he would not look me in the eye. That was when reality really set in. The second time I saw Dr. Bond was after my daughter, Katie's, first surgery when she was six days old and on life support. Her blood was being oxygenated by a machine circulating it out of her body and back in. He made some eye contact! It told me that we were not out of the woods yet, but getting there.

Some time after the next operation to realign her digestive system, I was getting into my car, which was parked on a busy street, and heard a honk. A Mercedes stopped in the middle of traffic and the driver got out, and came around the vehicle. It was Sheldon. He walked over, gave me a hardy handshake, and looked me right in the eye. The tears started to flow because I knew we had done it. You could say that my faith in him led to the survival of my daughter.

This is not to say that, along the way, I did not have my doubts. My faith was tested several times. As I said earlier, some years later, my son asked me what was the worst thing that had ever happened in my life. I did not immediately answer, but thought about it. Finally, I got back with him and said, "Nothing." He pressed further, saying there had to be something. I simply said, "She didn't die; your sister didn't die." I had imagined her funeral several times in solitary moments while sitting in the parking garage at the hospital, literally wailing. It did not happen. The image was so real and nothing remotely compared to it.

Katie is fourteen years old now, plays on the basketball, archery and golf teams at school, and, by the way, has cerebral palsy, but as you can imagine, with all that she has been thorough, she does not let it stop her one bit.

Exercise 12-a:

Do you have faith in yourself?

Exercise 12-b:

Identify ways that you can increase your faith in yourself. ☐

Exercise 12-c:

Do you have faith in others (your family, your co-workers, any organization you are a member of, your teammates, your doctors, etc.)?

Faith in a Higher Power

What can I write about the role of one's higher power in the pursuit of success that has not already been written? It has a real and significant place. One beyond comprehension. One of my favorite realizations has to do with Parkinson's. I often end my inspirational presentations to Parkinson's audiences by asking the rhetorical question, "Do you know why God allowed me to experience Parkinson's disease? Because He knew that I could handle it." I truly believe that. I believe that everything happens for the best. No qualifiers. There is a plan. Our mission is to do the best we can to fulfill that role to the best of our ability.

I love the expression, "Let go and Let God." What it means to me is that, you do the work (assess, envision, identify the steps, put forth the effort, prepare, practice, gain experience, develop contacts, etc.), you need to recognize that you don't have total control. There is a higher power that has a plan. As the country song goes, "Thank God for unanswered prayers." I like to say, "Everything happens for the best." We may not know what it is at the time, but it will probably reveal itself eventually. For me, I had a hard time, at first, seeing how my having Parkinson's is for the best. But it is. I am living a much more rewarding and purposeful life now, and it all has to do with my Parkinson's. To go back to the New Orleans mouse story, I live life to the fullest 'cause *I ain't dead yet.*

Exercise 12-d:

Do you believe in and have faith in a higher power?☐

Exercise 12-e:

If you believe in a higher power, identify ways that you can increase your own faith in that power.☐

Seat of the Soul

There is a great book by Gary Zubov entitled, *The Seat of the Soul.* The premise of the book is that our soul lives on after our current existence ends. This existence is labeled our personality. Each personality exists to obtain certain experiences and learn from them. Young souls have not had many personalities, while old souls have had a substantial number.

My best friend from college battled cancer for some time. I was able to stay in touch with Brad even though he was in Florida and I was in Kentucky. When I was not visiting him, we communicated by phone and text. I felt compelled to share parts of Zubov's book with him.

The book asserts that, if you do not learn what you are intended to learn during a particular personality, you are destined to repeat that personality and not move on to the next one. This revelation provides me some comfort now that I am getting older, and every day inching closer to death. As you have read in this book, I have gone to a whole new level to make sure my life has purpose. My purpose, in a nutshell, is to support my family and help others through my words and actions.

With Brad, his only concern was whether he made a difference. Did his life have purpose? I know it did to me and my observations were that it did to his parents, sons, friends Kevin and Shari, and even his ex-wife (who came to visit him with their sons the Christmas before he passed). Having a purpose can be as simple as a kind gesture; you may have no idea the effect of such a gesture. Brad's life had purpose.

I met Brad the first day of my sophomore year in my new dorm. I enjoyed my freshman year, but never felt like I belonged. I went to a state school in Massachusetts even though I grew up in New York. Many of the students had their friends from high school, and had little need to make new friends. At first, the new dorm felt the same as the one I was in freshman year, and I was ready to quit school. Then I met Brad. He was clearly the leader of the Attleboro, Massachusetts, group. I will never forget how he included me in their group from the start. It was a small gesture that meant the world to me. I told this story to him the night before he passed, and at his memorial. I am blessed to have known him.

Chapter **13**
Applying the Twelve Action Steps

"Believe you can and you're halfway there."

—Theodore Roosevelt

Put it all together: Apply the *Decide Success* principles. Here are some illustrative examples of ways you can utilize these steps.

Elevating Business to the Next Level

What could I do, as CEO of a successful organization, to increase or further enhance the success of the organization?

Decide Success

(1) Assess:
Take a hard look at your people. What attributes do you need to be present in at least one member of your top management team for your organization to be successful in your specific business? Operational, marketing, research, information technologies, or accounting expertise? Are these attributes present in your existing team? Some. What are the weaknesses of your team? Not enough divergent viewpoints. All have similar backgrounds and experiences. What are the strengths of your team? Stability and consistency of approach.

(2) End-vision:
What's your timetable: one year, three years, five years, ten years, twenty years, fifty years? When you project yourself into the future, what is the best imaginable picture? What does it feel like? Is there a taste to it? A smell? For example, in five years: open a plant in five additional states in the Midwest. Specific necessary actions: identify new business to support the plants, identify logically friendly locations to buy existing or build new plants, put together a project team, etc.

(3) Effort:
Your people have their "regular" full-time job. Do you have ownership from your people to put out the extra effort necessary to take on this project? If not, get it.

(4) Prepared:
Is there enough data available for the project team? If not, obtain it.

(5) Intense:
Do you have true buy-in that this expansion is the right decision, direction for the company and in the company's best interest? If not, debate it. Consensus through conflict is what a co-worker used to call it.

(6) Experiences:
Have members of the team done such a project before? If not or not enough, bring in additional resources. Specialists.

(7) Contacts:
Do we know who we need to obtain permission from to complete the project, how do we get in front of each

decision-maker and what is the best approach?

(8) Awareness:
We have continually asked why we need these plants and our response has consistently been that we do. Our competitors are not moving in this direction, but we are confident that we are seeing beyond what is apparent.

(9) Instinct:
If we don't expand, we are anticipating that, based upon our projections and judgment (instincts), we will run out of operational capacity in two years.

(10) Attitude:
We are not oblivious to the risks, but have weighed all factors and have a very positive attitude about the project.

(11) Integrity:
The team understands the standard of uncompromising integrity.

(12) Faith:
As the CEO, I have faith in my team, business and myself.

Here is another illustrative example.

Applying the Decide Success Principles: Reducing Injuries

What can I do, as corporate safety officer, to decrease the number and severity of injuries at fifteen steel processing plants across the United States, Canada and Mexico by ten percent a year for the next ten years within a reasonable budget?

(1) Assess: Weaknesses
I have done all that I can think of; I am out of ideas. Strengths: I have the commitment of upper management. Interests: I care about people and love the safety field.

(2) End-vision:
Feeling the pride of presenting a bar chart to the CEO and executive committee that shows decreasing injuries, even with an increasing number of employees. Seeing the smiling faces of the executives. Accepting handshakes and pats on the back. Walking through the plants knowing that you were involved in a program that allowed virtually all these fellow employees who you care about to go home from work uninjured. Not having to make "the call" to a loved one informing them of a serious injury or even death.

(3) Effort:
I am asking the question because I am willing to get out of my comfort zone and put out the effort necessary to prevent injuries from occurring.

(4) Prepared:
I have significant experience, but know that there is always more preparation that can be done.

(5) Intense:
I am committed to make this happen.

(6) Experiences:
I need to obtain "out-of-the-box" training. Get away from the "same old, same old."

(7) Contacts:
This is a fertile area for success. I have numerous contacts and resources. I have to tap into my safety resources for novel approaches. I need to touch base with my contacts in the safety field.

(8) Awareness:
The first step is for me to recognize that I am out of ideas and that insanity is defined as doing the same thing over and over yet believing that you will get a different result. Find programs that help me question what is and help me see beyond what is apparent.

(9) Instinct: Resistance
Change is uncomfortable and people don't like to be uncomfortable. Anticipate that you will meet resistance.

(10) Attitude:
There will be set-backs. As a famous actress once said, "Never let them see you cry." Commit to be the cheerleader. Stay positive. Your cause is a noble one.

(11) Integrity:
Do it the "right" way. Never doctor or spin any results or outcomes. Tell it like it is.

(12) Faith:
Trust your purpose.

Success Principles in Practice: Child's Life-Threatening Medical Condition

What could I possibly do to save my daughter's life?

(1) Assess:
I am an attorney with some medical training (former EMT).

Weaknesses: Have health insurance through work, but not significant excess funds to pay for procedures not covered by insurance.
Strengths/Talents/Abilities: quick study, excellent at expressing myself, charming, kind, big heart, likeable.

(2) End-vision:
My daughter coming home from the hospital swaddled up in my arms. Placing her in a car seat in the back of my green Explorer parked on the first floor of the parking garage near the exit door. The engine running and fully warmed up with the heat on. It is cold outside as I exit into the garage holding Katie closer to my body so she is not exposed to the cold between the building and the car. I envisioned this occurring months before it did.

Identify specific necessary steps: I have included these throughout the remaining steps.

(3) Effort:
Whatever it takes. Do extensive research on Katie's condition. Search for novel or experimental approaches in the literature. Determine which doctor/hospital is the best of the best. Spend as many hours with Katie at the hospital as I can physically manage.

Work nights, weekends, whenever to do my job, and improve Katie's chances of survival.

(4) Prepared: Exhaustive Diligence

Ask questions, lots of questions. Ask doctors, ask interns, ask technicians, ask nurses (especially nurses), ask the cleaning crew if you think it may help. Do my own web-based research so that I will know what to ask in the limited time I have with these professionals. Write out well-worded questions to be as efficient as possible with their time.

(5) Intense:

Find out what I can do to maximize the chances of my daughter's survival and then do it. Decide who will care for my daughter. What can I do to motivate the caregivers selected to provide the best possible care— go above and beyond?

(6) Experiences:

Identify other families who have had children with this same condition and survived. Interview each to determine any lessons learned from the experience. I thought of contacting families of children who did not survive and what they might have done differently, but did not because of the pain it would surely cause them and my ability to emotionally handle the contact.

(7) Contacts and Resources:

Louisville is a small town and it's relatively easy to make great connections. I am on the board of the Make-a-Wish foundation. Having Parkinson's, I have gotten to know many doctors and other medical personnel.

(8) Awareness:

Just as there are great lawyers and not-so-great lawyers (said as politely as possible), there are great doctors and not-so-great ones. I contacted all the doctors I knew to determine who they said was the best pediatric surgeon.

I also became aware of the ones who are the primary caregivers: the neonatal intensive care unit nurses. Fourteen years later and I still remember them: Nancy Gray, Nancy Allgood, and Susan Harris. Although I knew that they cared very deeply about all the babies, I wanted them to have a personal relationship with Katie through their relationship with me. I was the most charming, caring, kind, feeling, considerate person I could be with them.

They suggested that, although I could not hold her, hearing my voice would be beneficial. I made a tape of my voice and some my favorite soothing songs. I had to depend upon the nurses to flip and start the tape when I was not there. Did it help? Maybe. I can tell you that she knows every word to the Allman Brothers' song on the tape: "You're my blue sky, you're my sunny day, Lord you know, you make me high when you turn your love my way, turn your love my way ... hey ... hey."

(9) Instinct:

I needed something special for the nurses to really bond with me, and through me, with Katie. I heard that Bruce Springsteen was coming to a small venue in Louisville. I contacted the theater, explained what we were going through and asked if they could set aside eight great seats for me to buy when they went on sale. They agreed. I surprised the seven nurses who cared for Katie with tickets to see the Bruce, The Boss, third row.

(10) Attitude:

Positive, positive, positive. Although, as I said earlier, I could not help imagining her funeral at one point, 99.9 percent of the time I was absolutely convinced that Katie would live. Everyone around me could feel the positive energy emanating from my very being. I was not being strong, putting up a front, whatever; I truly was positive that my baby was a fighter.

(11) Integrity:

I don't want anyone to think that I expected any nurse to pay more attention to my daughter to the detriment of any other neonatal ICU baby. That never entered my mind. I just wanted them to give the best care possible to all the patients, including Katie. Further, the Springsteen tickets were to show my appreciation for all they do. Give them a shot in the arm (excuse the pun) to continue providing exceptional care. On the other hand, I would feel funny about giving each an envelope of cash instead even if it was the equivalent of the concert ticket price.

(12) Faith:

Finally faith—faith in the nurses, in the doctors and in my baby. Faith in God. I prayed a lot and still do. I firmly believe that the reason this happened is because God knew we could handle it. Just as with my Parkinson's. Everything happens for a reason. God knew we could handle it.

Exercise 13-a:

Complete your own *Decide Success* plan:

(1) Assess:
(2) End-vision:
(3) Effort:
(4) Prepared:

(5) Intense:

(6) Experience:

(7) Contacts:

(8) Awareness:

(9) Instinct:

(10) Attitude:

(11) Integrity:

(12) Faith:

Summary

"Great spirits have always encountered violent opposition from mediocre minds."

—Albert Einstein

"He who is not courageous enough to take risks will accomplish nothing in life."

—Muhammad Ali

MAPPING PHASE

(1) Conduct an extensive assessment focusing upon interests, abilities, talents, strengths, and weaknesses.

(2) Experience your own end-vision by actually projecting there and engaging all your senses, identify the specific necessary steps to make it your reality.

WORK PHASE

(3) Put forth your absolute best effort—be resilient.

(4) Prepare and practice until you are ready, then prepare and practice more—be diligent.

(5) Be so intense that you can feel a rush of adrenaline—be persistent.

ACTIVE PHASE

(6) Continually seek out challenging experiences.

(7) Identify, develop, and nurture extensive contacts and resources.

EXPANSION PHASE

(8) Increase your level of awareness by (a) actively listening, (b) continually questioning what is, (c) seeing beyond what is apparent, (d) proactively

anticipating, and (e) learning from mistakes.
(9) Get in touch with, and trust, your instincts.
LEGACY PHASE
(10) Exude the most positive attitude possible.
(11) Live up to a standard of uncompromising
integrity.
(12) Have faith in yourself, in others; in a higher
power and that believe your life has purpose.

There it is. Decide to be more successful. Decide to succeed. *Decide Success.* Follow these *Twelve Action Steps to Achieve the Success You Truly Desire* and *YOU WILL* be more successful. You will also be the best *you* that you can be and live a life that you love. You may even make a difference in the world and create your own legacy

It is not going to be easy; nothing truly worthwhile is. As M. Scott Peck writes, "Discipline is the basic set of tools we require to solve life's problems. Without discipline, we can solve nothing." Be disciplined. *Decide Success.*

You don't have to be successful in everything you do. Pick and choose. Prioritize. Keep a balance. Set aside time to smell the roses and enjoy the sunset. Even while you are engaged in these *Decide Success* twelve steps, continually remind yourself to relish the journey as well as celebrating when you reach the destination.

I wish you the best of success now and in the future. It is all up to you. *Decide Success.* And always remember *You Ain't Dead Yet!*

About the Author

John M. Baumann JD, BBA, is a writer, inspirational speaker, University of Louisville College of Business faculty member and practicing attorney. John is also caregiver to his teenage daughter, Katie, father to his college sophomore son, Joe, chair of the Make-A-Wish Foundation board of directors in Kentucky, and a self-proclaimed *Proud Person with Parkinson's.*

John contributed to the book *Roadmap to Success*, which also contains contributions by Dr. Ken Blanchard and Deepak Chopra. John earned his juris doctorate degree from Cornell Law School after graduating *summa cum laude* with a bachelor's degree in business administration from the University of Massachusetts School of Management. Mr. Baumann passed the bar and practiced law in Texas, Louisiana, and New Jersey before becoming general counsel of a NASDAQ listed corporation headquartered in Kentucky.

John has made an appearance as a commentator on CNN Headline News, has hosted an Internet talk show on success (with more than 50,000 monthly listeners), and was admitted as a full member of the National Speakers Association his first year of eligibility. As *The Inspiring Esquire*, John has produced two DVDs (*Learn Success Today* and *Learn Negotiation Today*) and a CD (*Reclaiming Posi-spective*).

John is a trial attorney specializing in employment, labor and general contract law. John is a workshop facilitator and consultant in workplace harassment elimination and union avoidance (*ProactivePreventionCulture.com*). John also helps employers properly work with employees who become disabled and represents employees whose employers do not treat their employees properly.

John has cherished being caregiver to his daughter (who has flourished despite being born with life-threatening birth defects and cerebral palsy) and is positively living with his own diagnosis of Parkinson's Disease since the ripe young age of forty-one. He is particularly proud of being selected the Most Inspiring Professor by the University of Louisville Scholar—Athlete of the Year. John dedicates his energy and passion to inspiring others and teaching success to audiences around the world.

To contact John for to speak at your event, or to see his current speaking schedule visit his website at:

www.JohnBaumann.com

To email John and share your thoughts about his book:

JohnDecideSuccess@gmail.com

To visit John's website scan the QR code below:

Speaking Reviews for Mr. Baumann

"Your personal stories of growth and optimism struck a deep cord with those in attendance. If motivation was your only goal, you succeeded. However, if you were striving to inspire deep belly laughter, internal reflection, misty eyes, and a healthy dose of "open your eyes to the world that surrounds" as they say in Hollywood, you nailed it!"
—Amy McNeil, SARC Executive Director

"...telling people your life story and your daughter, Katie's story, you could CHANGE lives...I was listening, I remember I cried, I laughed, I felt sad, and then happy, but at the end BEING STRONG, a much stronger person....as you were talking I was reflecting on my own life, on my own challenges. I found myself coming out of that session being a much stronger person."
—Shahin Shoostari, Ph.D., Conference Speaker

".... you came, you thrilled, you brought people to tears, you brought people to laughter, but, most importantly, you inspired."
—Kathleen Crist, Executive Director,
Houston Area Parkinson's Society

"Thank you for what you are doing - keep up the good work!! "You ain't dead yet"!! I've told that story several times since Saturday!!"
—Linda Cole, Immediate Past President,
Parkinson's Association of Alabama

"We met last week at Pritikin where I heard your inspiring motivational talk. I have read your book and wrote a review on Examiner.com where I am a travel writer. Keep up the good work you are doing for others and keep striving for yourself. You are an inspiration. I, and several others, have commented on what a good team you and Bernadette are together.
—David Jennings,
Baltimore Destinations Travel Examiner

"How To Make the Most Out Of Your Life – And Find Fulfillment Every Step Of The Way." Back by popular demand! When University of Louisville Professor John Baumann first spoke at Pritikin two months ago, guests stood up and cheered. His inspiring story of living (no thriving!) with Parkinson's Disease has motivated thousands to live their lives to their fullest.

—Donata Davis
Pritikin Longevity Center + Spa Marketing Coordinator

Made in the USA
Monee, IL
13 February 2020